ʻIke Ulana Lau Hala

Published by University of Hawai'i Press
in association with

Hawai'inuiākea School of Hawaiian Knowledge
University of Hawai'i at Mānoa
Dean Maenette K. P. Ah-Nee Benham

Volume Editors: Lia O'Neill M. A. Keawe,
Marsha MacDowell, and C. Kurt Dewhurst
Managing Editor: Lilinoe Andrews

Editorial Board
Maenette K. P. Ah Nee-Benham, Jonathan K. Osorio,
Puakea Nogelmeier, Lia O'Neill M. A. Keawe, Lilinoe Andrews

Advisory Board

Hawai'inuiākea is available online through
Project MUSE (http://muse.jhu.edu).

Hawai'inuiākea No. 3

'Ike Ulana Lau Hala
The Vitality and Vibrancy of Lau Hala Weaving Traditions in Hawai'i

Edited by
Lia O'Neill M. A. Keawe, Marsha MacDowell,
and C. Kurt Dewhurst

Hawai'inuiākea School of Hawaiian Knowledge

University of Hawai'i Press

Honolulu, Hawai'i

Library of Congress Cataloging-in-Publication Data

'Ike ulana lau hala : the vitality and vibrancy of lau hala weaving traditions
in Hawai'i / edited by Lia O'Neill M.A. Keawe, Marsha MacDowell, and
C. Kurt Dewhurst.
pages cm — (Hawai'inuiakea ; no. 3)
English and Hawaiian.
Includes bibliographical references.
ISBN 978-0-8248-4093-8 (pbk. : alk. paper)   1. Lauhala weaving—Hawaii.
2. Hala tree—Utilization—Hawaii.   I. Keawe, Lia O'Neill M. A., editor
of compilation.   II. MacDowell, Marsha, editor of compilation.
III. Dewhurst, C. Kurt, editor of compilation.   IV. Title: Vitality
and vibrancy of lau hala weaving traditions in Hawai'i.
V. Series: Hawai'inuiakea monograph ; 3.
TT877.5.I54 2014
746.4209969—dc23
2014002381

Cover image: *Nā'ū nā kala*
by Marques Hanalei Marzan

Printed by Sheridan Books, Inc.

We honor the wisdom of our kūpuna, we celebrate the efforts of current practitioners who continue this ʻike, and we look to future generations who will keep the traditions of this art form alive.

Contents

Color photographs follow page 114

From the Dean

Welina Mai!

The Hawaiʻinuiākea Series is a collaborative endeavor. With each volume, our special editors work with authors—scholars, cultural practitioners, students, and elders—to capture the creative and intellectual power of an important topic. I have been insistent on this collective approach, although it is quite time consuming and labor intensive, because the journey invites authors to write together and to engage in critical dialogue with reviewers, which serves to strengthen the written voice. What we have learned from the process of producing three volumes thus far is that this method of collaborative writing, reviewing, and revising has elevated Kanaka ʻŌiwi critical thought, illuminated artistic expression, and honored the knowledge of our kūpuna.

In this, our third volume, the coeditors lovingly query, make sense of, and present the life force of our people through the art and craft of ulana lau hala. These are culture-specific voices, experts in their multidisciplined fields of scholarship and practice—all essential to revealing the symbolic significance and relevance of an art form that is both utilitarian and beautiful. What is woven into these pages is a reminder of what some of us may have forgotten or not understood until we come to the place where a weaver's skillful hands take up the plaiting of our moʻokūʻauhau/genealogy. In both a metaphorical and practical sense, ʻike ulana lau hala presents the vitality of those who have passed and the spaces that are still warmed by their breath.

Similar to our prior volumes, we present thought in both ʻōlelo Hawaiʻi and English, the voices of youth and kūpuna, the work of scholars and practitioners, and artistic expression.

While Hawaiian orthography may on occasion differ from piece to piece, it is our commitment to honor the sources from which these texts originate, which may sometimes include a directive to keep the written style as is, with no changes. Readers will be reminded of the historical value of lau hala as well as its contemporary significance, will be introduced to the movement to restore the vibrancy of ulana lau hala, and will be put on notice that the environmental threat to our endemic hala is here! Personally, I am grateful that we were able to include Uncle Roy in this volume and am reminded that there are many kūpuna voices that we still need to record. Indeed, this volume should press each of us to ask this question: "Are we doing enough to care for the stories and art forms of our kūpuna?" The hope of the Hawaiʻinuiākea editorial board and the special editors of this volume is that we collectively foster a sustainable and healthy ulana lau hala movement.

Naʻu me ka haʻahaʻa,
Maenette K. P. Ah Nee-Benham, dean
Hawaiʻinuiākea School of Hawaiian Knowledge
University of Hawaiʻi at Mānoa

Editors' Note

Just as a community of individuals and a great deal of time are necessary to grow, harvest, and prepare raw materials, then learn and teach the knowledge required to ulana, the work of many hands over several years was necessary to create this volume about lau hala[1] and its role in Hawaiʻi. Like the moe and kū of hala that are intertwined in the art of ulana,[2] there are strands of knowledge that have come together, with collective concentration and united effort, to form this book about this art that has had such an important place in the tangible and intangible heritage of Hawaiʻi, an art that is a fundamental part of being Hawaiian.

While so many strands of knowledge and partnerships have been integral to today's understanding of the place of lau hala in Hawaiian identity and culture, this volume presents some specific relationships worth noting. The authors of the pieces included here are affiliated with The Bernice Pauahi Bishop Museum (Honolulu), the Hawaiʻinuiākea School of Hawaiian Knowledge at the University of Hawaiʻi at Mānoa (Honolulu), and the Michigan State University Museum (East Lansing, Michigan). Each of these organizations is concerned with the engagement of communities in the process of documenting, presenting, and interpreting cultural knowledge as well as facilitating a greater scholarly and public awareness of that knowledge. All three institutions have a commitment to working with and for Indigenous communities to address social justice and well-being issues for Indigenous peoples. This book serves as an extension of our collaboration together and with community-based partners.

Each contributor has come to this project because she or he seeks to advance knowledge and understanding about lau hala and, by doing so, will help address contemporary needs of sustaining and strengthening the traditional knowledge associated with lau hala. Each contributor has traveled her or his own path in the process of preparing to ulana our knowledge together. This volume, *ʻIke Ulana Lau Hala: The Vitality and Vibrancy of Lau Hala Weaving Traditions in Hawaiʻi*, is a result of our united interests and reflects both our individual and collective experiences with ulana. The book embraces contributions informed by diverse scholarly disciplines based on oli, mele, spoken-word poetry, oral histories, first-person narratives, historical photographs, archival records, and expressive visual arts. In that variety it appropriately reflects the diversity and richness of lau hala and its place in Hawaiian history and life.

Lia O'Neill M. A. Keawe, University of Hawai'i at Mānoa
Marsha MacDowell, Michigan State University Museum
C. Kurt Dewhurst, Michigan State University Museum

NOTES

1. "Lau" in the Hawaiian language means "leaf." The term "lau hala" refers to the leaves of the *Pandanus tectorius* or screwpine.
2. To plait or weave.

A Note on the Cover Art

E 'ohana kākou

Ulana binds us to each other, continually weaving our families together into a great mat. This dynamic network grows with every new relationship, beginning with our foundational strands that sparked the flame of creativity, the source of our traditions and values, which continue to pass on to overlapping layers. Though breaks occur over time, which extinguish individual flames, the light continues to endure. Remembering that our choices determine our mat's growth and stability is vital. We all must choose.

The skills that ulana is built upon recall a time when patience, humility, perseverance, and excellence were part of everyone's values, a time when perpetuation of one's practices was a priority. But with the passage of time, these priorities ebb and flow and continually conform to the fashion of the present. Those who choose to go against the current of the present and hold fast to the values of a different time maintain the ancestral link to our past, the flame that is carried from generation to generation.

Kuleana, one's right, privilege, concern, and responsibility, is the basis of understanding ulana. The privilege of embracing a legacy that has woven itself through the generations is a great honor few today accept, for it is also a burden. Bearers who assume stewardship of this flame become pillars of light within the community, celebrated for illuminating the way into the future, all the while charged with the sacred duty of ensuring the flame's transmission to the next generation. Will these lines be broken?

The final words on Kalaiokamalino's makaloa mat of protest, "Nau Na Kala," are depicted on the cover of this book in the form of a contemporary plaited piece, recalling a time of great change in the art form of ulana. It is a reminder that we must never forget where we come from and to honor all those who have come before us. This torch has been passed to us. Do we deprive the voices yet unheard of this gift? Who among you will don this mantle of ancestral memory?

Do you accept?
Nāʻū nā kala.
The forgiveness resounds.
ʻEliʻeli kau mai.

Marques Hanalei Marzan

Ka Mele No Ka Ulu Lauhala O Kona

Aunty Elizabeth Maluihi Lee (2010)

Haāheo nei, na lau
O Ka Ulu Lauhala
E ulu nei, me ka oli oli

Mahalo ia nei
Na aā lau loa
Me na lala, Hīnano, ki hala

I mili mili i a ana
Me kealoha
Mai ka puuwai
E pulama ia ana mau

Chorus:
Puana ia ana
Mai ke kumu hala
E hoolana, mau ana
No Ka Ulu Lauhala
E hoolana, mau ana
No Ka Ulu Lauhala
Lauhala

Aloha Ka Lau Pūhala

Katherine Maunakea (July 6, 1985)

Aloha i ka mamo,
O ka lau Pūhala,
A he lei laulima nui,
Haʻaheo i ka hīnano,
Ua lohe ʻia i ka leo manu,
Hui pū ʻia me ka aloha,
No ka pae one,
Puni Hawaiʻi nei.

Eō ku nei o Niʻihau,
Pā aku me Lanaʻi,
Hui pū aʻe me Kauaʻi,
Neʻe mua me Molokaʻi,
Huli mai ka moku i Maui,
Hoʻi hou nei me Oʻahu,
E hoʻohui ʻāina,
Puni Hawaiʻi nei.

Kaulana ka hui ʻāina,
Poina ʻole e na Kupuna,
ʻEleu hou me ke aloha,
He makana ʻiʻo nui,
Hoʻoulu like ka manaʻo,
No ka lau o ka Pūhala,
E pono no na ʻōpio,
Puni Hawaiʻi nei.

Pua ana i ka mamo,
O ka lau Pūhala,
A he lei laulima nui,
Haʻaheo i ka hīnano,

Aloha to a Gem,
The lau, the Pandanus,
A lei of many hands,
Splendor is the hīnano,
Voices of birds are heard,
Linked together with Aloha,
On the sandy shores,
For all of Hawaiʻi nei.

With an answer from Niʻihau,
Also from Lanaʻi,
Linked together with Kauaʻi,
Moving on to Molokaʻi,
Then sail to Maui,
Again, return to Oʻahu,
Linking all islands,
All for Hawaiʻi nei.

Famous are the island gatherings,
Forget-not those Kupuna,
Alert again with Aloha,
With their gifts and ideas,
Together our thoughts may grow,
For the lau of the Pandanus
Make right for our young ones,
For all of Hawaiʻi nei.

Bloom out with this Gem,
The lau, the Pandanus,
A lei of many hands,
Splendor is the hīnano,

Ua lohe ʻia i ka leo manu,
Hui pū ʻia me ke aloha,
No ka pae one,
Puni Hawaiʻi nei.

Voices of birds are heard,
Linked together with aloha,
On the sandy shores,
For all of Hawaiʻi nei.

Ka Ulana Kaulana

R. Kekeha Solis

As important as continuing the tradition of ulana lau hala (weaving lau hala) is the tradition of using 'ōlelo no'eau (wise sayings or proverbs) of our kūpuna. This chapter presents the brilliance of kūpuna in weaving words. It is my great hope that readers will be inspired to continue this tradition as well.

Ke no'ono'o a'e i ke 'ano ulana 'ana i hele a kaulana ma kēia pae 'āina a puni, 'o ia nō paha ka ulana 'ana i ka moena pāwehe o Ni'ihau, ka ulana 'ana ho'i me ka makaloa. Mai kahiko mai nō ia 'ano ulana 'ana. A i kēia mau lā, he kāka'ikahi paha kona 'ike 'ia, akā, 'o kekahi 'ano ulana 'ana i hele a kaulana, 'o ia ka ulana 'ana i ka pāpale 'ānoni. He keu ka nani o ia 'ano pāpale ke nānā aku.

He mau 'ano ulana nani nō ia, akā, 'o ka ulana kaulana e kau a'e nei i luna i po'omana'o, 'a'ole ia 'o ka ulana 'ana i ka makaloa a i ka lau hala a mea 'ē a'e paha. 'O ke 'ano ulana e mana'o 'ia nei, 'o ia ka ulana 'ōlelo, 'o ia ho'i, ka 'ōlelo no'eau, 'ōlelo kahiko, a 'ōlelo kaulana ma kekahi 'ōlelo 'ana.

Ke Akamai Ulana 'Ōlelo

'O nā kūpuna o kākou, ua nui ko lākou 'ike ma ka ulana 'ōlelo. Hō'ike mai ka mea kākau o ka mo'olelo nūpepa "Ke Ano O Na Olelo Hookaau,"

> Hohonu no paha ka olelo a na kupuna o kakou, e hiki ole ai ia kakou ke ike iho i ka manao oia mau olelo. O ko lakou ike kamailio he hohonu . . . E ike iho ana nohoi kaua e ka makamaka heluhelu i ke akamai o na Hawaii ma na hoopilipili olelo ana. Nui no ka ike. (1939)

A he mōakāka ka hohonu o ka 'ike kama'ilio i hō'ike 'ia ma ke 'ano o ke koho 'ia 'ana o ka hua 'ōlelo a me ka mana'o. Penei ka 'ōlelo a kekahi mea kākau, "Ke hoomanao iho nae oe e ka mea heluhelu i keia mau olelo, mikioi ke kiiia ana. Auhea la na olelo a na lahui e aku i hiki e hoopili mai i keia mau olelo Hawaii? Aole loa! Aole wale no he nani i ka hoolohe ana a ka pepeiao, aka, he maikai ke kii manao ana" ("Kekahi Mau Olelo Hawaii Naauao," 1922). A e 'ike 'ia ana nō ia maika'i o ke ki'i mana'o 'ana ma hope iki aku. I kekahi manawa, 'o ka nani o ka pāwehe, ua ho'onalonalo 'ia, e like me ka 'ōlelo a Kilau Pali, "O ka hohonu o ka manao iloko o kekahi hopunaolelo i manao ole ia, he ano nui ia olelo, o ia ka noeau" (1922). A i kekahi manawa, ma muli o ka mākaukau loa ma ka ulana 'ōlelo 'ana, he pōkole wale nō ka 'ōlelo e like me ka mana'o o ka mea kākau nāna kēia 'ōlelo, "Aole paha he olelo ma ke ao nei, i like mai me ka olelo Hawaii, ka loaa o ka manao iloko o na huaolelo pokole loa. I keia mau mamalaolelo e ikeia ai ka naauao o na kanaka o ke au kahiko" ("Kekahi Mau Olelo Hawaii Naauao," 1922). A no laila, he mea maopopo wale ka nui o ka 'ike o ko kākou mau kūpuna ma ka ulana 'ōlelo.

Akā 'o ka mea minamina, e like me ke kāka'ikahi o nā kānaka ulana moena pāwehe a loea ulana lau hala, ua kāka'ikahi ihola nā loea ulana 'ōlelo. Penei ka mana'o o ka mea kākau o "Kekahi Mau Olelo Hawaii Naauao,"

> Eia nae ka mea aloha, mawaho ae o na kanaka i oo, aole lohe hou ia aku o keia mau olelo, a aole no hoi e loaa ana ka manao i kekahi poe o keia au o kakou. . . . Aole no paha he manawa e pau loa ai keia olelo, aka, e hoea mai ana nae ka manawa, e lilo ai ka olelo i olelo hou, o ia hoi e nalowale ana ka nani o ka olelo, a e lilo aku ana i olelo hapa-Hawaii. I keia mau la no e nee nei, ke lohe aku oe i na keiki e olelo mai ana, ua like me ka olelo ana a na kanaka o ko na aina e. Aole hoi o kela olelo pahee, nani, elike me ka'u i lohe ai i ko'u mau la kamaiki. (1922)

Ma ka 'ao'ao pōmaika'i, 'a'ole i nalo loa nā loea ulana 'ōlelo. Hō'ike 'ia kekahi mau loea ulana 'ōlelo ma ka puke 'o *Place Names of Hawai'i,*

> Not many years ago Mary Kawena Pukui found a colleague, Ke=oho=kapu, hard at work. Instead of the banal comment that a haole would make, she asked cryptically, "E kū'o'i a'e ana i ke One=o=Luhi?" (Are [you] limping along the Beach of Weariness?) Ke=oho=kapu, quick as a flash, said resignedly, "He pi'i-na kē-ia i mauna Pa'u-pa'u." ([I'm] just climbing up Drudgery Hill.) Both were pleased, and as a result of this repartee, the work may have seemed less like drudgery. The core of these sayings is the double meaning—in the place names Luhi "weariness" and Pa'upa'u "drudgery"—a device rarely used in English sayings. (Pukui, Elbert, me Mookini, 1974, 'ao. 266)

A 'a'ole wale nō 'o lāua, akā, he mau mea hou aku nō. He nui nō nā kūpuna i 'oki leo 'ia. 'O kekahi, 'o ia nā kūpuna i lilo i hoa kipa no Ka Leo Hawai'i, ka polokalamu lekiō 'ōlelo Hawai'i, a i ninaninau 'ia ho'i e Kauanoe Kimura. 'O kekahi po'e kūpuna, ua ninaninau 'ia e Clinton Kanahele. 'O kekahi, ua ninaninau 'ia e Mary Kawena Pukui. He nui nō nā kūpuna i ho'opuka i ka 'ōlelo no'eau, a e hō'ike 'ia kekahi ma 'ane'i. 'O Kakae Kaleiheana kekahi kupuna i akamai loa ma nā ʻōlelo kahiko. I kona manawa e kipa ana iā Ka Leo Hawaiʻi ma ke ʻano he hoa kipa, e kamaʻilio ana ʻo Momi Wong i kekahi hoa kupuna ma ke kelepona, a ʻōlelo akula ʻo ia nei, "Ke aloha nō paha kēia, kāhea aku nō au iā ʻoe i kekahi manawa, cause, hoʻi ana au, kali mai ana paha kēia poʻe kamaliʻi iaʻu, lōʻihi maoli nō kēia luahine i hele aku nei, ʻaʻole i hoʻi mai" (Kaleiheana, 1975). A i ka manawa a Kakae Kaleiheana i lohe ai i ia mau ʻōlelo a Kupuna Wong, hoʻopuka maila ʻo ia i kahi ʻōlelo, " ʻO ia ka ʻōlelo a kahiko, hele ʻāina ʻo Pīlali" (Kaleiheana, 1975), me ka hene aku nō hoʻi o ka ʻaka. A ma hope mai o ka haʻalele ʻana iho o Kupuna Wong, nīnau akula ʻo Kauanoe Kimura i ia ʻōlelo a Kupuna Kaleiheana i hoʻopuka ai. A wehewehe maila ʻo ia, "Ke hele a ʻaʻohe noʻonoʻo e hoʻi . . . hele naʻaupō, ʻaʻohe noʻonoʻo aʻe, he hana paha ko ka hale, e hoʻi paha, kali ʻia mai ana paha" (Kaleiheana, 1975). Kohu mea lā, ua paʻa loa nō ia ʻōlelo a kahiko, ʻoiai, ʻo ka paʻa ia e hoʻopuka ʻia ai i ka wā kūpono.

Eia mai kekahi moʻolelo no ke kupuna akamai i ka ʻōlelo noʻeau. E ninaninau ana ʻo Clinton Kanahele iā Rose Manu. Haʻi aʻela ʻo ia i ka moʻolelo o kekahi kanaka ʻili kou a me ke kuhihewa ʻana o kekahi luahine, he Pāʻele ʻo ia. Penei ka haʻi ʻana mai o Kupuna Manu i ka moʻolelo ma ka leo o ua kanaka ʻili kou nei, me he mea lā, nāna e moʻolelo mai ana.

> Hoʻokahi lā, ma Kona au, hele au e holoholo ma kahakai, kēia luahine e noho ana ma waho o ka lānai o kona hale . . . mea mai nei nō hoʻi, auē e pouli ana hoʻi kākou, aia naʻe, ʻaʻole ʻaʻole pouli kēlā lā, so, huli aku nei nō au pane aku nei au iā ia . . . ʻaʻole, aia nō ka lā e kau nei . . . hilahila loa kēlā luahine, hoʻi ʻo ia i loko o kona hale. (Manu, 1970)

Aloha nō kahi ʻili kou i ka hoʻohenehene ʻia e kahi luahine. A aloha nō hoʻi kahi luahine, ʻo ka hele a hilahila loa i ke kuhihewa, he Pāʻele kahi kanaka ʻili kou, a ʻaʻole maopopo iki ka ʻōlelo Hawaiʻi iā ia. He Hawaiʻi kā ua ʻili kou nei. ʻO ka nani naʻe, ʻo ka hiki i ua luahine ala ke ulana i ka ʻōlelo no ka pōuli.

A ʻo ke akamai ulana ʻōlelo i ʻike ʻia aʻela ma luna aʻe nei, ʻo ia ke akamai ma ka ʻike kamaʻilio a me ka hoʻopilipili ʻōlelo paha. ʻEā, ʻo ia mau kumu alakaʻi i hōʻike ʻia aʻela ma luna, he mau ʻōlelo ia na kahiko, a ulana ihola ua mau kūpuna nei i loko o ke kamaʻilio ʻana. ʻO kekahi akamai ulana ʻōlelo, ʻo ia ka haku ʻana i ka ʻōlelo noʻeau. A ʻoiai he puke kēia no ka lau hala a me nā mea e pili ana, no laila, e nānā iki kāua e ka makamaka heluhelu i kekahi mau ʻōlelo noʻeau e pili ana i ka lau hala a me ka pū hala paha.

He nani nō ka ulana ʻia ʻana o ka pū hala a me kekahi māhele paha ona i loko o ka ʻōlelo noʻeau a kahiko. Penei kekahi, "He lau hala lana" (Pukui, 1983, 80). He ʻōlelo kēia no ke kanaka ʻaeʻa, e ʻauana ana mai ʻō a ʻō, a he ʻaeʻa haukaʻe paha. A ʻo kekahi manaʻo i hōʻike ʻia ma ka puke wehewehe ʻōlelo Hawaiʻi, ʻo ia hoʻi, he ʻuko ʻole ke kanaka i kūamuamu ʻia i ka lau hala lana, me he lau hala e lana ana ma ke kai (Pukui me Elbert, 1986, 196). ʻO nei ʻōlelo noʻeau, he lau hala lana, ʻaʻole ʻōlelo ʻia kahi e lana ai ka lau hala. Inā ma ke kai e lana ai, he maikaʻi ke koho ʻia ʻana o ka lau hala, ʻo ia ka mea lana, ʻoiai, he paʻa nō ia lau e lana hele ai i nā wahi like ʻole. A inā aia ka lau hala i ke kai, he makehewa nō, ʻaʻole hiki ke ulana ʻia. He mikioi nō ke kiʻi manaʻo ʻana.

He nui nō nā ʻōlelo noʻeau e ulana ʻia ana ke ʻano o ka pū hala a me kahi māhele paha ona. Eia kekahi, "He pū hala aʻa kiolea," ʻo ia hoʻi, he kanaka nāwaliwali (Pukui, 1983, 99). ʻO ka pū hala, ʻaʻole paha ia he lāʻau i paʻa loa i kona mau aʻa, e like paha me ke ʻaliʻi kū makani. Ma muli paha ia o ke ʻano o ke aʻa, he kiolea, a ʻo ia ka mea e lilo ai nei ʻōlelo kahiko i ʻōlelo kūamuamu, a i hoʻokomo ʻia ai hoʻi i loko o ke oli hoʻonāukiuki a ka makuahōnōwai kāne o Kawelo i ka manawa a ke kaikamahine i kiʻi aku ai i ka hāuna lāʻau. A penei kahi māhele o ia oli:

E o e ku ka hauna laau a kaua i ko kane,
He kolea ko kane, he wawae liilii,
He ulili ko kane, he holoholo kahakai,
Paia e ke kai nui, e hina wale ana no,
He nui pumaia ko kane, ku ikaika,
He puhala ko kane, he aa kiolea. ("Ka Moolelo o Kawelo," 1908)

Ua ulana nani ʻia nō kahi oli o luna aʻe nei. A e like me ka ulana ʻia ʻana iho o ka pū hala a me kona ʻano i loko o nā ʻōlelo kahiko, pēlā nō i ulana ʻia ai kekahi mau manu, ʻo ke kōlea a me ka ʻūlili a me kekahi mea ulu, ʻo ka pū maiʻa. A ʻo ia mau mea, he mau mea nāwaliwali nō. ʻO ke kōlea, he wāwae liʻiliʻi kona, ʻo ia hoʻi, he wīwī kona wāwae. ʻO ka ʻūlili, he holoholo kahakai, a i ka manawa e pā ʻia ai e ke kai nui, ʻo ka hina aku nō. A ʻo ka pū maiʻa, he hiki wale ke kulaʻi ʻia aku a hina. Aloha nō kahi Kawelo i ke kūamuamu ʻia. Ua nani naʻe ke kiʻi manaʻo ʻana.

Eia mai kekahi ʻōlelo no ka hala, ke kī hoʻi, o ka ʻāhui hala, a hōʻike pū ʻia kahi māhele o ka moʻolelo o Hiʻiakaikapoliopele, kahi hoʻi i puka ai ua ʻōlelo noʻeau nei. Penei ka moʻolelo,

No keia lilo ana o Wahieloa ia Pelekumukalani, ua naauauwa iho la o Pele (i honua-mea) i ke aloha o kana kane "o na la heu ole," wahi a kahiko, "ka mea nana i wehe ke pani ke ki o kau makemake." Pale ka ai, ka ia ame ka wai iaia. Ua hele mai la ke aloha o nei mea he kane a haakohi i na onohi maka. (Poepoe, 1908)

He aha lā ka manaʻo o ua ʻōlelo nei a kahiko, ʻo ia hoʻi, "ka mea nana i wehe ke pani ke ki o kau makemake"? Haʻi maila ʻo Kauka Noʻeau Warner no kona manawa i hele aku ai i mua o Kupuna Josephine Lindsey me ka nīnau 'ana aku no ia 'ōlelo (ma ke kama'ilio 'ana). A wahi a Kauka Warner, i kona ho'opuka 'ana aku i ia 'ōlelo, hene wale a'ela nō ka 'aka a ke kupuna, a 'a'ohe ona wahi 'ōlelo a ho'opuka mai (ma ke kama'ilio 'ana). 'O ko'u kuhi, i hene a'e ka 'aka a Tūtū Lindsey no ka pili o ia 'ōlelo i ka hana le'a o ke kulu aumoe, 'o ka ho'oipoipo 'ana. Ma mua, e kuhi ana ko 'oukou mea kākau, 'o ia pani, 'o ke pani wai ia o uka, a ke hemo aku, kahe akula ka wai. Akā, i ka 'ike 'ana aku i kekahi mana'o o pani i loko o ka puke wehewehe, 'o ia ka hala o ka 'āhui hala, aia i lalo o ka 'āhui (Pukui me Elbert, 1986, 314). A 'o ke pani, ke hemo mai, he hemo wale nā hala, nā kī ho'i, i koe ('o ia wahi like nō). A no laila, ke kuhi 'ia nei, he pili ia 'ōlelo no'eau i ke kī o ka 'āhui hala.

I kekahi manawa, ulana 'ia ka hana a kahiko i loko o ka 'ōlelo no'eau, 'o ia ho'i, ke ho'omaopopo 'ia ka 'ōlelo no'eau, ho'omaopopo 'ia kahi hana i kuluma i nā kānaka. Penei ia 'ōlelo "Puna maka kōkala" (Pukui, 1983, 301). 'O ka hana a nā kūpuna i ulana 'ia, 'o ia ke kanu 'ia 'ana aku o ka 'īewe o ke keiki 'akahi nō a hānau, ma lalo o ka pū hala i lō'ihi mai ka lihilihi maka o ia kama iki, e like ho'i me ke kōkala o ka lau hala ('o ia wahi like nō). E kau a'e paha ka nīnau, no ke aha i ulana 'ia ai 'o Puna i loko o nei 'ōlelo. No ke aha lā? 'O ko Puna wale nō ke kanu i ka 'īewe ma lalo o ka pū hala? 'O Puna wale nō kahi i kaulana ai ka maka kōkala? Ma ka *Moolelo Hawaii o Pakaa a me Ku-a-Pakaa*, amuamu akula 'o Kūapāka'a i ke ali'i o Puna iā Huaa i ka maka kōkala lau hala, "Holo ae nei nae o ua o Hua-a, o ua alii hoi o makou o Puna, aohe nae hoi he alii, he kaukau alii no, he maka kokala lauhala no Puna" (Nakuina, 1902b, 'ao. 44). No Puna wale nō paha ka maka kōkala lauhala. A i 'ole, he hiki paha ke ho'okomo 'ia kekahi 'āina i kaulana i ka lau hala kōkala nui.

Ma ia 'ōlelo i luna a'e nei, ulana pū 'ia ihola ka inoa 'āina, a he mea ma'a mau nō paha ia. Eia mai kekahi 'ōlelo kaulana loa no Puna a me ka hala, "Puna paia 'ala i ka hala" (Pukui, 1983, 301). Ua kaulana nō 'o Puna i ka paia 'ala i ka hala, he kuhihewa nō paha kekahi, e like me kahi 'elemakule ma ka mo'olelo Hawai'i 'o Kalapana ke keiki ho'opāpā. I ka 'ōlelo 'ana a'e o Kalapana, "He keiki keia no Puna, no ka paia ala i ka hala" (Nakuina, 1902a, 19). Pane mai kekahi 'elemakule, "He kaena hoopunipuni nae, he polopolona no hoi paha ka paia o ko lakou hale la e like me ko kakou, o ka pa mai nae o ke ala o ka hinano a po ae la ka aina a puni i ke ala o ka hinano, alaila, lawe olelo wale ae no ke keiki o Puna, he paia ala i ka hala ko Puna" (Nakuina, 1902a, 19). A wehewehe akula ke keiki, 'o Kalapana,

He ala, he aina ala o Puna,
Noho iho la na keiki kupa o ka aina,
A pala mai la ka hala,
Ooki iho la i ka pua a kui ae la,

A lei ae la i ka a-i,
Ala aku la ka po a aumoe,
Ooki mai la ka hiamoe,
Kau ae la na lei hala i ka paia,
A pela i kapaia ai ko'u aina,
O Puna paia ala i ka hala—e. (Nakuina, 1902a, 20–21)

A wehewehe maila 'o Mary Kawena Pukui, i ka wā kahiko, e ho'okomo 'ia ka polohīnano i loko o ke pili o ka hale pili, i mea e 'a'ala ai 'o loko (Pukui, 1983, 301). He nani nō ka wehewehe 'ia 'ana mai o ia 'ōlelo 'o Puna paia 'ala i ka hala. 'O ko 'oukou mea kākau kekahi e kuhi ana, he 'ōlelo ho'ohālike wale nō ia, kohu paia paha ke 'ala ma muli o ka paoa mai o ka hala. 'A'ole pēlā, he paia 'i'o nō ia i 'a'ala i ke 'ala o ka hala.

'O kekahi 'ōlelo kahiko, e hō'ike mai ana i ka pilina o ka pū hala me ka i'a o ke kai. "Pala ka hala, momona ka hā'uke'uke" (Pukui, 1983, 284). Ua maka'ala nō nā kūpuna, a 'ike a'ela lākou, i ka manawa e pala ai ka hala, 'o ia nō ho'i ka manawa e momona ai ka hā'uke'uke. A 'o kekahi aku, "Pala ka hala, momona ka uhu" (Pukui, 1983, 284). A 'o ka pilina o kēia, 'oiai, momona ka hā'uke'uke, a 'o ia nō ka mea 'ai 'ia e ka uhu, 'o ka momona pū ia o ka uhu.

Eia mai kekahi 'ōlelo, "Moena hāunu 'ole o ka nahele" (Pukui, 1983, 236). A he nani kēia. He pili nō i ka ulana 'ana. 'O ka hāunu, 'o ia ka ho'okomo 'ana aku i ka mau'u lau hala i kāu mea e ulana ana a poepoe ai ka mea e ulana 'ia ana. 'O ka moena hāunu 'ole o ka nahele, 'a'ohe hāunu. He wahi moena i hana 'ia me ke kupukupu, ka lau o ka mai'a, a 'o kekahi lā'au ulu o ka nāhelehele. A i kekahi manawa, 'ike 'ia ua 'ōlelo kahiko nei i ka ulana 'ia i loko o ke mele a kanikau paha, e like me kahi kanikau no Kupa Maila, penei kahi lālani o ia mele, "Kuu kane i ka moena haunu ole o Lilikoi" (Maila, 1876).

'O ka mea hope a kākou e nānā aku ai, he nane. E ha'i mai i ku'u nane, "Kuu wahine, eha piko" (Judd, 1930, 88). He aha lā ka ha'ina? 'Ehā piko o ka wahine? 'Ekolu wale nō piko o ka wahine. 'O ka manawa, 'o ka piko, a me ka ma'i. Akā, e like me ka mea ma'a mau, he ho'ohālike ka nane. 'A'ole ka ha'ina he wahine. 'O ka ha'ina, he pili nō i ka ulana 'ana, 'o kekahi mea ho'i e ulana 'ia, 'o ia ho'i ka moena lau hala. A moena lau hala lā, pehea e moena lau hala ai? Penei, 'o ka hua 'ōlelo no kekahi o nā piko o ka wahine, 'o ia ho'i, 'o ke kohe. A 'o kekahi mana'o o kohe, 'o ke kihi ia o ka moena. A he 'ehā nō kohe o ka moena. A 'o ia paha ka mea i ho'ohālike 'ia ai ka wahine ma kēia nane. 'O ke kohe, he ma'i no ka wahine.

'A'ole o kana mai ka nani o ke ki'i mana'o 'ana o nā kūpuna. Ua mōakāka nō i ka nānā 'ana aku nei i ia mau 'ōlelo kahiko e kau a'ela ma luna. He nui ka 'ike kama'ilio a he akamai ho'i i ka ho'opilipili 'ōlelo 'ana. A he nui hou aku nā 'ōlelo no'eau e like me nā mea o luna e pili ana i ka pū hala a me kona mau māhele. Akā, ua lawa paha ia e 'ike ai i ke akamai ulana 'ōlelo o nā kūpuna.

Ka Ulana ʻAna I Ka ʻŌlelo

Ua nānā ʻia aku nei ka ulana ʻana aku o nā kūpuna i ka ʻōlelo noʻeau ma luna aʻela. A ʻo ia nō kahi ʻōlelo paipai aku a ko ʻoukou mea kākau, ʻo ia hoʻi, e ulana aku kākou i ka ʻōlelo noʻeau mai nā kūpuna mai i loko o kā kākou kamaʻilio ʻana i ko kākou hoʻōla ʻana i kā kākou ʻōlelo aloha. A i mea ia e nani ai kā kākou kiʻi manaʻo ʻana, a e hohonu ai hoʻi ko kākou ʻike kamaʻilio. A he hana maikaʻi nō hoʻi e hahai ai i ke ʻano noʻonoʻo ʻana o nā kūpuna.

Piha hauʻoli ka naʻau o ko ʻoukou mea kākau i kahi lono i paʻē maila i ka pepeiao no kahi kumu kula kaiapuni, ʻo Jonah Chang Purdy ka inoa, nāna e aʻo nei i kāna mau haumāna (papa mālaaʻo a papa ʻekahi paha) i nā ʻōlelo noʻeau like ʻole, a ʻo ka mea i ʻoi aku ai ka hauʻoli, he ulana nō kāna mau haumāna i ka ʻōlelo noʻeau i loko o ko lākou kamaʻilio ʻana ma waho o ka papa, ma ka pīpā alanui a ma ka hale paha. Ua kuʻi nō ka lono o ia mau hana a pā ka pepeiao o ko ʻoukou mea kākau. Wahi a Kauka Noʻeau Warner, no nā makahiki he 23, ʻaʻole nō i nui ka hoʻopuka ʻana o nā keiki o ke kula kaiapuni i ka ʻōlelo noʻeau. I ia mau makahiki, ua aʻo ʻia nō kekahi mau ʻōlelo noʻeau, akā, he aʻoaʻo ke ʻano. Eia mai kekahi, mai makaʻu i ka hana, e makaʻu naʻe i ka moloā. ʻO ia paha ka mea i ulu ʻole ai ka hoi o nā keiki (Warner, ma ke kamaʻilio ʻana). A i kēia mau lā, aia nō nā keiki kaiapuni ke hana nei i ka ulana kaulana a nā kūpuna, ʻo ia hoʻi, ke hoʻopuka nei lākou i ka ʻōlelo kahiko a nā kūpuna.

E Wehe ʻIa Ke Pani Ke Kī O Ka Makemake

Ua kamaʻilio ʻia aku nei kekahi o nā ulana kaulana o ka ʻāina, ʻo ia hoʻi ka ulana ʻōlelo ʻana a nā kūpuna a loaʻa ka ʻōlelo noʻeau a me ka hoʻopuka ʻia ʻana aku o ia mau ʻōlelo i ulana noʻeau ʻia. He mea maʻa mau ia mai nā kūpuna mai, a heleleʻi liʻiliʻi, ʻaʻole naʻe i nalo loa. Ua mahalo ʻia nā kānaka o Niʻihau, ke hoʻomau akula nō i ia mau hana nani. A pēlā nō e hoʻomau ʻia nei ma ʻō a ma ʻaneʻi o kēia pae ʻāina. A ke lana nei ka manaʻo o ko ʻoukou mea kākau, e laha loa nō kēia ulana kaulana o kēia pae ʻāina. Mahalo i nā kūpuna nāna i hoʻoili mai i nā ʻōlelo kahiko i o kākou, a mahalo hoʻi iā ʻoukou i ka hoʻomau ʻana i ia mau ʻike.

NĀ MEA I KUHIKUHI ʻIA

Andrews, Lorrin (1974). *A dictionary of the Hawaiian language.* Japan: Charles E. Tuttle.

Judd, H. P. (1930). *Hawaiian proverbs and riddles.* Honolulu: The Museum.

Kaleiheana, K. (1975, ʻApelila 13). ʻO L. K. Kimura ka hoʻokipa [Ma ka lola, HV24.94A]. Ka Leo Hawaiʻi, Ka Hui Aloha ʻĀina Tuahine (Prod.). Moore Hale, ke Kulanui o Hawaiʻi ma Mānoa.

Ka Moolelo o Kawelo. (1908, Kēkēmapa 18). *Kuokoa Home Rula,* ʻao. 2.

Ke ano o na olelo hookaau. (1939, ʻApelila 26). *Ka Hoku o Hawaii,* ʻao. 4.

Kekahi mau olelo Hawaii naauao. (1922, Mei 18). *Ka Nupepa Kuokoa*, 'ao. 2.

Kekahi mau olelo noeau a na kupuna. (1922, Kepakemapa 28). *Ka Nupepa Kuokoa*, 'ao. 7.

Maila, M. K. (1876, Iulai 13). He kanikau no Kupa Maila. *Ka Lahui Hawaii*, 'ao. 3.

Manu, R. (1970, Iulai 30). 'O C. Kanahele ka ho'okipa [Ma ka mp3]. Clinton Kanahele Collection. Joseph F. Smith Library, ke Kulanui 'o Berigama Iana—Hawai'i.

Nakuina, M. K. (1902a). *Moolelo Hawaii o Kalapana ke keiki hoopa-pa*. Honolulu: Grieve Publishing Co.

Nakuina, M. K. (1902b). *Moolelo Hawaii o Pakaa a me Ku-a-Pakaa*. Honolulu: Kalamakū Press.

Poepoe, J. M. (1908, Ianuali 10). Ka Moolelo Kaao o Hiiaka-i-ka-Poli-o-Pele. *Kuokoa Home Rula*, 'ao. 1.

Pukui, M. K. (1983). *'Ōlelo No'eau: Hawaiian proverbs and sayings*. Honolulu: Bishop Museum Press.

Pukui, M. K., me S. H. Elbert (1986). *Hawaiian dictionary: Hawaiian-English, English-Hawaiian* (rev. and enlarged ed.). Honolulu: University of Hawai'i Press.

Pukui, M. K., S. H. Elbert, me E. T. Mookini (1974). *Place names of Hawaii*. Honolulu: University of Hawai'i Press.

'Ike Pāpale: Lau Hala in Hawaiian Cultural Heritage

Marsha MacDowell, C. Kurt Dewhurst, and Marques Hanalei Marzan

The mana [supernatural or divine power] that we put into our [lau hala] things, whether they are traditional or contemporary, is Hawaiian. . . . We weave, we put our aloha, we talk story to them, we laugh, we cry, we sing, we dance, because that's who we are.[1] E. Kawai Aona-Ueoka

Hula, poi, aloha shirts, the Hawaiian Shaka, quilts, mu'umu'u, slack key guitar and 'ukulele music, surfboards, and lū'au are well known around the world as contemporary symbols of Hawai'i's local culture. Lau hala is less known outside of Hawai'i, but among many Native Hawaiians, lau hala is an important symbol of Hawaiian identity.[2] Photographic records, oral histories and recordings, and the oral transmission of knowledge document that hala is a plant that is deeply entwined in the tangible and intangible cultural heritage of Hawai'i. The art of lau hala—the weaving—turning the lau (leaves) of the hala (pandanus palm) into mea ulana (woven objects) is fundamental to the craft and art of this treasured cultural heritage practice. For some practitioners, making and using lau hala makes them feel connected to this place, Hawai'i, and to others who weave lau hala.

Lau Hala in Hawaiian Cultural History

Weaving lau hala [pandanus leaves] is like weaving a relationship. . . . It is weaving together the older with the younger generation. . . . We are all connected through weaving.[3] Gladys Grace

Puna, kai nehe i ka ulu hala. (Puna, where the sea murmurs to the hala grove.)[4] author unknown

In Hawai'i the hala tree, *Pandanus tectorius,* also known as screwpine, formed extensive coastal forests, and travelers on land or water could orient themselves by the smell of the hala wafting from groves, some of which were famous. For instance, along the coast in Puna on Hawai'i Island, the region known as Puna paia 'a'ala i ka hala (Puna hedged with fragrant pandanus) has long been celebrated in oli and mele. Land with hala became treasured property of families.[5] References to the fragrant hala, 'āhui hala (the fruit of the hala tree), and lau hala abound in historical and contemporary chants, songs, dances, and stories. In one oli, the canoe of Pele, the volcano goddess, became entangled in hala roots when she first arrived in Hawai'i. Pele was so angry that she tore the roots into many pieces and threw them as far as she could; wherever the pieces landed, new trees then grew.[6] Another oli tells of a hidden spring underneath a hala tree located where the Punahou School of Honolulu now stands.[7] Yet another describes a hala tree that grew to be a kupua (super-natural being); it had grown from a seed from a mythical hala tree from Puna called Manu'u-ke-eu that Pele's brother carried to Hawai'i and planted.[8] Prov-erbs, riddles, and sayings allude to hala and lau hala.[9] The roots and seeds were used in traditional medicines, as food, for cordage, and to make lei that are traditionally given to individuals at points of transition in their lives.[10] Be-cause the word "hala" also means gone, slipped away, and missed, and can refer to a mistake, a hala lei is sometimes given at New Year's to bid farewell to past grudges: Ua hala ka makahiki (the old year has slipped away).[11]

Dispersion of the Hala by Madame Pele by Dietrich Varez. Image courtesy of Dietrich Varez.com.

The leaves of the hala are long and tapered, varied in width and color, and pliable to different degrees and are the predominant plaiting material in Hawai'i and the greater Pacific. Indeed, the sails of the vessels that carried early inhabitants to and from the islands were fashioned of woven lau hala panels sewn together with olonā.[12] Ancient custom was to bury Hawaiian royalty in caves along with some of their most precious possessions, and lau hala mats have been found in some of those ancient burial caves.[13] Before the introduction to the islands of prefabricated items, lau hala and makaloa[14] were used to fabricate sleeping and floor-covering mats, pillows (uluna), walls and ceilings of homes, carrying and storage baskets, fans, clothing, and an array of objects that were used in everyday and ceremonial practices from paying taxes to ritual gift giving.

Mats were made for many specific uses with particular sizes, shapes, and weaving styles for these uses. Coarsely woven mats were used on dirt floors or to cover stored food items. Finer mats were made for items like hikie'e (beds), which used a long, continuous mat wound back and forth on a bed frame to serve as a mattress.[15] Two-foot-square lai, or salt mats, were used during the summer months to collect sea salt. According to twentieth-century lau hala researcher Edna Williamson Stall, "these mats were weighted and placed in depressions on certain beaches where the ocean would wash over them and deposit salt."[16] She reports that when the salt was dry it was put into hala baskets

Early depiction of lau hala sails by John Webber, ca. 1780, artist on Captain Cook's voyage to Hawai'i.

with a heavy lid and the baskets were then placed in dry caves. Stall also describes mats used by Hawaiian men in their wrestling matches; during the match men clasped hands and then tried to move each other off the mat.[17] Another form of weaving sometimes called Nuʻa is now almost gone. Four examples can be found at the Huliheʻe Palace. In this method, twelve- to eighteen-inch-high walls of lau hala were built up from a base and then flaps covered a space in between, which was filled with lau hala scraps or ferns—thus creating a soft, fragrant cushion.[18] Letters of the alphabet were sometimes incorporated into a mat, especially when the mats were intended as gifts. One sleeping mat "was inscribed 'Kuʻuipo' (My darling), 'Kuʻu lei' (my crown), 'Kuʻu milimili e' (my pet)."[19] In at least one known instance, in 1874 a makaloa woven mat was even used as a means of protest when the mat maker inscribed text, made of letters formed of strips overlaid onto the mat's warp and weft, to petition King Lunalilo to lift the tax imposed on owners of livestock, work animals, and pets.[20]

In addition to the knowledge about the historical use of mats that has been passed down through oral transmission, the use of woven items was observed by some of the earliest explorers, traders, and missionaries from the Western world. Indeed, as early as 1778 Captain Cook gave accounts of plaited goods of lau hala, makaloa, bulrush, and other materials.[21] As indicated by an 1877 newspaper account, while the practice was still widespread, already there was concern that coming generations would no longer be weaving in their homes: "In the past days, Hawaiian women plaited mats of bull rushes, lauhala, and makaloa which last made pawehe mats. Some women are still making them to cover their floors and beds, but the younger generation now growing up will not know these fine arts that will be useful in their homes."[22]

According to various accounts, the making and use of plaited items continued to flourish well into the nineteenth century but began to ebb toward the last quarter of the century due to a number of factors associated with the influences of a growing non-Hawaiian population.[23] Yet some twenty-first-century weavers have memories of lau hala mats being used in homes into the twentieth century and even to the present day. Marcia Omura, for instance, remembers, "when I was growing up, lau hala mats were still in use. . . . However, . . . families began using linoleum, and later . . . wall-to-wall carpet."[24] She goes on to reflect on some of the reasons why few individuals now use mats in their homes:

> I suspect lau hala mats began to fall out of grace (or began to get less popular) simply because of the novelty, easier maintenance and/or comfort of wall-to-wall carpet vs. lau hala mats. Perhaps it became less popular as weavers themselves were giving up the art, succumbing to the convenience of such newer technologically savvy materials. . . . People had to go to work because the cost of living was

going up, up, up which of course created a vicious cycle of buying more things instead of dropping back to a traditional lifestyle, which incorporated or relied on people making things they needed.[25]

Because weaving is often a therapeutic activity, it has been used in hospitals and other places of healing. For instance, tuberculosis patients at the Kula Sanatorium on Maui and at the Samuel Mahelona Memorial Hospital on Kaua'i were encouraged to learn lau hala weaving.[26] Even today, a number of weavers report that weaving contributes to their health and well-being.

While the plaiting of lau into mea ulana occurred throughout the islands, weaving lau hala into pāpale (hats) became a particularly prevalent activity in the South Kona area of Hawai'i Island. There were many pāpale makers among the Japanese, Chinese, and Native Hawaiians who worked the ranches and the coffee plantations on the island of Hawai'i. Sturdy baskets of woven lau hala reinforced with wire and rubber strips became an important tool for coffee pickers. A form of basket for shipping coffee was also developed in Kona and was in use through at least the middle of the twentieth century; one basket forms the bottom and a second basket fits snugly on top, forming a cube.[27] Children learned early how to weave and families supplemented their income by making and selling hats.[28]

Today, woven lau hala items are still used by Hawaiians in ways that are both culturally specific and claim a Hawaiian identity; lau hala continues to be a fundamental element of the Hawaiian personal and public cultural land-scape. The use of woven lau hala is one of the elements that mark the "Hawaiian-ness" of the event or place or person. Hula dancers, paniolo (cowboy ranchers), church choir members, and individuals participating in or attending Hawaiian cultural events regularly wear pāpale or other decorative personal adornments, including purses, hat lei, and apo lima (bracelets). The cultural importance of lau hala continues to be recognized today through its use in creating the con-

Ed Kaneko with a lau hala basket for picking coffee beans. Image courtesy of Kris Kaneko.

Pāʻū rider in paniolo parade. Photo by Sherry Blanchard, courtesy of Cherie Okada-Carlson.

tainers needed to bury the remains of Native Hawaiians whose original burial sites were excavated by archaeologists or were in areas disrupted by military, civic, commercial, or private construction.[29]

Mea ulana today is used by many individuals in many places and ways throughout Hawaiʻi—as yoga mats, to create pencil holders, desk in-boxes, wastebaskets, flower vases, carrying bags for computers, and covers for cell phones and water bottles. Woven lau hala is used to cover almost any surface including lobby walls in hotels, mirror and picture frames, slippers, car dashboards, visors, and sun reflectors. Facsimile lau hala is printed on wrapping paper, notepads, mouse pads, wallpaper, and fabric. Tattoos of lau hala weaving designs are also popular. Master artist and kumu Pōhako Kahoʻohanohano has tattooed lau hala designs on his hands, feet, arms, and legs, which, although he jokes that he always has his reference materials literally on hand, indicates his seriousness and dedication to his art.[30] As Pōhako explains, "All my tattoos have to do with hala and weaving. Tattoos are part of our [Native Hawaiian] culture. One of my tattoos honors my seven female kumu who have taught me. . . . [It has] seven woven koana (strands) of hala. Another tattoo is a design that comes from a kumu. It is known as ʻeke kaimana (bag of diamonds). It is a piko (center) pattern viewed from both sides, negative and positive."[31] Some of the patterns came to Pōhaku in dreams. Long after he had one of

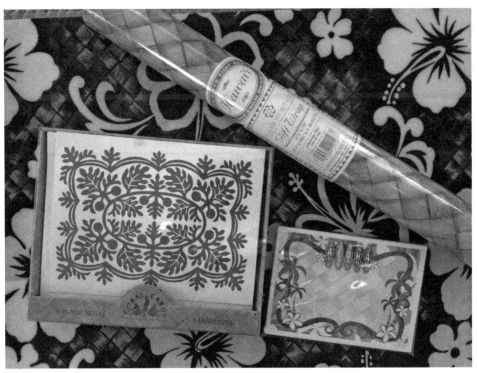

Examples of commercial items. Image courtesy of Marsha MacDowell.

these patterns tattooed on him and was using it in his work, he learned that it was one of his grandmother's favorites.[32]

Lau hala is also used by some individuals to create sculptural forms that are simply personal artistic expressions. Imaikalani Kalahele and Duncan Seto are wonderful examples of Hawaiian artists who incorporate lau hala into their work, taking the material to another level of conceptual complexity. Kalahele entwines lau hala into anthropomorphic figures, imbuing his work with the essence of the material, while Seto plaits three-dimensional objects, speaking to the issues Hawaiians face today.[33] Hāliʻimaile "Maile" Andrade is another artist who uses both traditional and new techniques to create work that pushes the boundaries of lau hala art. She was raised in a family that valued handwork and their Native Hawaiian cultural heritage, and she was a haumana of Elizabeth Maluihi Lee in the Folk Arts Apprentice Program of the Hawaiʻi State Foundation on Culture and the Arts. She also received arts training in universities and now is developing a Native Hawaiian Creative Expression Program at Kamakakūokalani Center for Hawaiian Studies at the University of Hawaiʻi at Mānoa. About her art she states, "My work reflects and is rooted in a native Hawaiian worldview. I would like to explore and question through contemporary art forms and visual statements the use and perpetuation of stereotypes from many lenses."[34] She explains further about the duality of her art, which is infused with both her own cultural heritage perspective and knowledge she has gained outside of that heritage:

> I think there's deeper understanding that comes from mastering a customary practice. When I'm weaving or I'm making kapa, I'm understanding that material. I'm understanding the process—how, why did they choose a certain process to go through to make this piece? What are the levels of thinking and seeing the world from their perspective? It puts me in a space that better connects me to who my ancestors were. Not so much the physical part, but more about how those processes happen in your head and in your naʻau, in your being. That understanding then allows you to take those same processes and conceptual ideas and move them to a contemporary material. You're doing the same thing, and that's what makes it Hawaiian.[35]

Hala and lau hala continue to be celebrated in contemporary chants, songs, dance, and other expressive arts such as fashion design. For instance, Johnny Lum-Hoʻs song "Puna paia ʻaʻala i ka hala" praises the many ways to use dried lau hala.[36] In his song "Wahine with the Lauhala Hat," John Leal paid tribute to a woman who makes and wears a plaited hat:

She's the talk of the town.
She's always around
The wahine in the lauhala hat . . .

You can see her every day,
Busy working away
Weaving lauhala mats and little lauhala hats[37]

A mele about lau hala hats, "Kuʻu Pāpale Lauhala," has also been recorded by several Hawaiian artists and interpreted by many kumu hula.[38] As recently as 2012, the Hālau Nā Pua Uʻi O Hawaiʻi danced *Kuʻu Pāpale Lauhala* and won second place in the 2012 Kupuna Hula Competition.[39] To celebrate the fifteenth anniversary of the annual Ka Ulu Lauhala O Kona gathering, founder and kumu Elizabeth Maluihi Lee composed and sang a mele about the importance of sharing knowledge about lau hala weaving.[40] Hilo-based artist and Hawaiian cultural specialist Sig Zane is known for his textiles and clothing with simple graphics that depict native Hawaiian flora and fauna as well as designs based on traditional Hawaiian material culture, including lau hala and pūhala. Zane encourages individuals to tend to the meaning of the plant when they wear one of his shirts. For instance, because "hala" can mean "mistake," he warns against wearing a shirt with hala when attending a wedding.[41]

Lau Hala and Cultural Knowledge

We cannot weave without lau niu [coconut palm leaves] or lau hala [pandanus leaves] or makaloa [sedge], or the aerial roots of the ie'ie [freycinetia]. We cannot practice our art without those plants. We are related to these plants. Our legends tell us that when certain of our plants disappear, we too, will disappear.[42] Sabra Kauka, 2005

Gathering leaves was done by both men and women but plaiting was women's work and their skillful fingers made not only the mats and sails but also pillows, baskets, fans, and later hats. Pandanus leaves, lau hala could be had at any time of the year and the best to use were those that had just become dry on the tree. The best time to prepare the materials was in the cool of the day, morning or evening, for the heat of [the] sun tended to harden the leaves making them less pliant to work with.[43] Mary Kawena Pukui, c. 1945

All lau hala weaving depends on the natural resource. Different trees have different traits, making them better suited to specific plaiting projects. Two general varieties exist, one having defensive thorns along the edges and spine of each leaf, while the other, which was introduced to Hawai'i from Tahiti, lacks thorns completely. Both varieties are used in plaiting, but some weavers have an affinity for one type over the other.[44]

Few individuals realize and internalize the knowledge and skills that are needed to know where suitable hala grows, how to harvest lau in ways that protect the hala, and how to process (i.e., clean, trim, sometimes cure, and then cut into strips) the lau into workable weaving materials. These steps are time consuming and require skills that can only be learned from practice. This knowledge is the basis of a weaver's development and growth. With a strong knowledge foundation, individuals can explore innovative solutions to obstacles as well as create new forms that are unique in today's weaving communities.

Pāpale

I live and breathe my art. . . . Cleaning of the leaves is done in the early mornings and harvesting in the evening. It is through this ritual, that a connection is made between the weaver and leaves, thus every hat, every item crafted, bears its own character, it[s] own uniqueness that can never be duplicated.[45] Lola Ku'ulei Spencer, 2012

When I was 10 years old, my grandmother taught me to make baskets for coffee picking. When I was a child, if you wanted to play, you had to weave first, because that's how our life was. We took our woven hats to the store to exchange for food, not money. A hat probably went for less than 30 cents. Every day after school I had to weave one ipu, and on Saturdays, had to weave six ipu before I could play.[46] Peter Park, 2005

I was about six years old when I started helping my mom pick and clean lau hala. It was one of [our] responsibilities to help our mom. There was no kaukau [food] if you don't do this don't do that. It was discipline. . . . We didn't get paid for our work, it was all for trade. Besides there was not much to buy in those days, kerosene, salt, and once a year, clothing. We would help my mother get enough materials to exchange for these things. . . . We exchanged our hats at the store [Kimura Store] and the store sold them to the plantation.[47] Elizabeth Maluihi Lee, 2005

Before the coming of the first foreigners to the islands in 1778, Hawaiians wore hats, usually of conical shape, only when working in the sun for long periods of time. With the introduction of Western clothing styles, Hawaiians became acquainted with hats and incorporated them into everyday and special occasion attire.[48] According to Stall, Hawaiian men were the first to adopt the Western style of hat wearing, and lau hala was plaited into the stovepipe style of hat worn by missionaries.[49] She also reports that when Hawaiian women began to adopt the custom of wearing hats, there was much creative activity among the weavers, and newly invented patterns were greatly respected.[50]

Through the making of hats, pāpale weavers were able to preserve some of the knowledge of the intricate plaiting that was being forgotten while incorporating new materials and technology. At the same time, new weaving designs, patterns, and hat styles have been continually developed to reflect artists' ideas and the fashions of the time. Today, weavers work to fill the demand for new forms, but they also look back to the older styles and try to reintroduce them into today's society. Marcia Omura remembers well her kumu's words about older ideas that were constantly being carried forward in ulana that seemingly appeared new: "Whenever I thought I was making something new, a new style, I'd show Aunty Gladys. She'd look at whatever it was I had made and simply say, 'My grandmother made that.' Four simple words just chock-filled with wisdom. On first glance, it might seem like a bona fide observational remark she was making. But over time (talking years!), I slowly began to understand Aunty Gladys' true meaning was to keep me humble, to remind me that others had come before me."[51]

Historically, two distinct styles of plaited hat making were done in Hawai'i, one of which has become the dominant practice of today's weavers, sometimes referred to as the Kona style. In the Kona style of hat making, an ipu, a wooden form or solid block, is used to form the crown of a hat. The ipu traditionally was made out of koa, mango, hau, olive, cherry, and banyan.[52] More recently, pāpale makers have been using Styrofoam wig forms or an ipu formed of laminated wood crafted and sold by skilled local craftspeople. South Kona native Herb Kaneko, now living in Pearl City, for instance, often attends gatherings of weavers so that he can supply them with his handmade ipu.[53] The top of the ipu is oval in shape and the overall circumference corresponds to the size of the finished hat; different shapes and sizes of blocks are used to create hats of various sizes and styles. Once the weaving is completed, the pāpale is put back on the ipu and lightly moistened. Simple or elaborate creases in the hat's shape are then made by hand or by pressing the dampened lau with a warm iron—a process called blocking.[54] A hat originally blocked one way can be reblocked to create an entirely new shape or style. The other primary technique used to make pāpale is known as pāpale 'ie, or the braided hat technique. It consists of sewing a long plaited strip, 'ie, into a hat shape. Few today practice this technique, but interest in the weaving community in how to make hats of this type is beginning to grow. Once a basic hat is finished, many kumu will admonish the maker or hat wearer that it should have a band or lei, which can be of twisted or braided lau, feathers, fresh or dried flowers, or anything that complements the hat or is suitable for the occasion on which it will be worn.

Hat styles have ranged from elaborately detailed to practical utilitarian.[55] Talented artists have created styles for which they have become known. For instance, Esther Westmoreland's open-weave pāpale with a square crown and a floppy brim was popular in the 1950s.[56] Margaret Lovett's cup-and-saucer hats are characterized by wide brims and intricate 'ānoni (two-tone) patterns; she also is credited with reviving the baseball cap style, and the form has become one of her signature styles. Even mistakes can creatively launch a style; in 2006 when Cherie Okada-Carlson inadvertently cut her hat, she made it into a unique airline stewardess hat. As she recalls, "We were doing baseball caps [under the instruction of Margaret Lovett] and I trimmed the koana (strips) too soon and the edge of the bill unraveled and I couldn't get it back together so Margaret reshaped it and salvaged it."[57] Ed Kaneko specializes in paniolo-style hats with high crowns. Special events or historical figures can serve as inspiration for hats. Michael Nāho'opi'i made a stovepipe hat similar to those Abraham Lincoln wore and, in 2010, several weavers began making fascinators, the type of millinery worn by some attendees at the wedding of Great Britain's Prince William and Kate Middleton. Many individuals make, buy, and wear lau hala pāpale because, as one commentator wrote in 2012, "Whether or not your head is cold, the fact is you look hotter in the right hat. . . . It's an investment, but each is handmade, usually by a lau hala master, and shows the world that you appreciate your culture as much as you enjoy looking good."[58]

Hat making involves skills that can only be learned by practice and with mentorship. While haumāna may learn from different kumu, generally they respect and attempt to perpetuate the teachings and stylistic traditions of one kumu. Weaving is considered an act of participating in the infinite wisdom that belongs to the kūpuna, the collection of kumu that have touched the lives of haumāna. Hāliʻimaile Andrade describes how weaving is informed not just by the steps necessary to weave, but, more importantly, by the very worldview of the weaver: "Our mana goes into it and our process of how we see the world goes into it, gives it a different kind of relationship to it. To us, it's not just an object. We need our own native perspective in how we view the world, how we tell others about who we are, because these are not just objects. . . . It is our kupuna."[59] Marcia Omura says that when she finished her first hat under the tutelage of Gladys Grace, she wanted to pay her kumu for the lessons. Aunty said, "I cannot take your money. We family."[60] Her words conveyed volumes about her worldview and, specifically, the relationship that was forming between her and Marcia, her haumana.

After learning how to gather, clean, and prepare hala, a haumana learns to make a piko, which in ulana means the center of the woven object but in Hawaiian also means the beginning or the place from which life begins.[61] Once the piko is learned, then the haumana can make a variety of items, mats, purses, and pāpale. The construction steps vary in approach depending on the technique, but this is where the aesthetic style manifests in the form of color, texture, shape, and patterning. A basic hat with no designs is typically done using a pattern known as maka ʻoʻeno (twill). After becoming proficient in this pattern, a weaver may learn other patterns to create uniquely patterned hats. Many traditional patterns preserved in pāpale have recorded names, usually referencing things in nature. Examples of named designs include honu (sea turtle), nēnē (geese in flight), and mauna (mountain). Other designs refer to manmade objects like lei hala (pandanus lei), papa konane (Hawaiian checkers), and hale (house). The use of multiple colors of lau hala, known as ʻānoni, in a hat is also a means to create unique designs.[62]

The tools for lau hala weaving have evolved over time as new technologies and materials have become available. Over the years many different tools and slight variations of techniques have been used. As Marcia Omura observed, "Kūpuna did not discourage their haumāna or new weavers from innovating or repurposing items as tools as long as the resulting weave was nice."[63] Many weavers today treasure the old tools passed on to them by their kumu, relatives, or found in yard sales—as they reflect the inventive and practical spirit of those who went before them. Common basic weaving tools in the first part of the twenty-first century include the ipu (a damp washcloth for cleaning the lau), a knife or scissors for cutting sections, a hiʻa (a little stick tool to push or pull the lau), water spray bottles to dampen lau while weaving, rubber bands and string to hold the pā (finished top of the hat) onto the ipu, a gauge for splitting,

Samples of hats from Aunty Harriet Soong's collection. Image courtesy of Marsha MacDowell.

a needle and thread for sewing, strippers, and rollers. Weavers today also often use hair clips and clothespins to keep their weaving strips tangle free and often bundle their tools and unfinished hats in soft cloth wrappers.

In preparation for weaving, lau must be cut into strips of uniform width, which varies depending on what product the weaver is making. For instance, a pāpale requires thin lau strips while a basket or mat uses wider strips. Weavers use a koe (stripper) to cut the lau into the desired width. Koe were originally fashioned from pieces of old metal cans or razor blades mounted at equal distance on pieces of wood, but most weavers today use specially made hand and box strippers. Each stripper usually has up to ten sharp blades, usually X Acto brand, mounted facing up at a sixty-degree angle. The setting of the blades is adjustable; they can be removed or respaced for cutting wider splints. The rectangular box stripper is designed for heavier-duty use and for safety as some even have Plexiglas tops over the blades for the safety of the weaver. Koa and other Hawaiian woods are often used for special strippers and are works of art themselves. Weavers continue to be inventive in creating new tools to assist in different steps of the weaving process. Peter Park, for instance, was renowned for his reengineering of machines for weavers' purposes, including rolling lau into kūka'a (rolls of dried lau hala) and stripping lau. Once he even adapted his motorized wheelchair so that when turned upside down, its motor ran a lau roller and stripper.

Passing on the Knowledge of Lau Hala

My kumu, Aunty Gladys Grace, says that for a weaver to be good, you have to give back. She wants us to take in the knowledge that she's passing on to us, but she also wants to pass it on to the next generation in a traditional way of learning.[64] Michael Nāhoʻopʻiʻi, 2005

In generations past, traditional knowledge and skills related to lau hala weaving would have been learned within the family or local community context. With the introduction of foreign influences came new contexts for learning as well as new activities that competed with cultural practices such as lau hala. As early as 1877, laments about the challenges to maintaining traditional weaving practices in Hawaiʻi were being voiced: "Let the young women combine the knowledge from their mothers with the new knowledge that comes from the haole [foreigners] and new teachers. Keep the hands occupied with work, the head with knowledge, and the inner person with thought. Learn that which you have and reach out for the new. Let the grandmothers teach their grandchildren to plait mats, twist cords, and sew."[65]

While learning lau hala in family and community contexts has been sustained, today there are fewer individuals who have the technical mastery and deep cultural knowledge of the art and, for a variety of reasons, kumu and haumāna often have little time to devote to teaching and learning. When the relationships between kumu and haumāna extend over time, haumāna realize and treasure that the knowledge shared is deep and rich.[66] The craft of turning a bundle of lau into a beautiful hat is only a small part of what is being learned; language, beliefs, protocols, aesthetics, songs, and stories are conveyed along with all the needed steps of creating ulana. Another weaver describes the knowledge he has gained from his seven kumu: "When I learned, I was one-on-one with my teachers. I went to their homes, became part of their family. You eat with them, weave with them. You grow up with them, their children, their great-grandchildren. [Today] I can look at a hat and know who made it by the color of the *lauhala* used, the style of the weave, the pattern. . . . To know the history and knowledge behind a piece is greater than just copying a design."[67] As two students realized, in becoming someone's student they are become the kumu's cultural progeny.[68] Haumāna respect and honor their kumu in many ways, including carrying on the teachings they have been given. Michael Nāhoʻopʻiʻi paid tribute to his kumu in an unusual way; he plaited the names of each into the hatband for his pāpale.[69]

Certainly there are a number of formal and informal learning contexts in Hawai'i in which learning lau hala weaving is important. In formal educational programs, lau hala weaving is part of many curricula from early childhood through university programs.[70] Dancers and chanters associated with hālau hula (hula school) learn the art as an integral part of their training as Hawaiian culture practitioners. More informal learning environments include community centers, museums (such as The Bernice Pauahi Bishop Museum), stores specializing in Hawaiian products (such as Nā Mea Hawai'i/Native Books in Honolulu), and many large hotels and resorts, which host demonstrations and classes in traditional Hawaiian arts, including lau hala weaving. The Hawai'i State Foundation on Culture and the Arts has also helped to perpetuate the transmission of lau hala knowledge through its traditional arts apprenticeship program.[71] The program has funded a number of kumu to work with apprentices one-on-one to advance the knowledge and skills of the haumana. Among the weavers who participated in the program as kumu or haumana were Lola Spencer, Elizabeth Maluihi Lee, Esther Makuaole, Minnie Kaawaloa, Jane Nunies, Lily Sugahara, Betsy Astronomo, Peter Park, Esther Westmoreland, Harriet Soong, and Gladys Grace.[72] Some haumāna went on to become kumu.

Because the number of Native Hawaiian skilled practitioners has remained relatively small and the number of kumu even smaller, several grassroots weaving organizations have formed to stimulate increased interest in learning lau hala weaving and to perpetuate the rich cultural knowledge associated with lau hala. 'Aha Pūhala, Inc., organized the first lau hala conference in 1987 in Hilo.[73] In 1997, Gladys Grace and Frank Masagatani founded Ulana Me Ka Lokomaika'i (to weave from the goodness within) on O'ahu.[74] During the late 1990s and early 2000s, an informal group met at the site of the old airport in Kona, and another group, led by Ed Kaneko, is associated with the Donkey Mill Art Center, Hōlualoa, Hawai'i. Ho'oulu Ke Ola O Nā Pua, 'Aha Pūhala O Puna, Ka Ulu Lauhala O Kona, and 'Ohi Lauhala are other groups active in

Aunty Gladys Grace and her haumana. Image courtesy of Marcia Omura.

the twenty-first century. Retreats held by these organizations or by individual kumu, for beginning and advanced haumāna, have also been critical to building a community of practitioners who can continue the art. As the announcement of one workshop states, "As always, everyone is welcome to come and enjoy being surrounded by all the accumulated knowledge of our group."[75]

One of the largest groups is Ka Ulu Lauhala O Kona, established in 1996 by Elizabeth Maluihi Lee. When the Office of Hawaiian Affairs in 1993 named Elizabeth a Living Treasure of Hawai'i for her contributions to preserving lau hala weaving, she said at the time that the art was disappearing and dying because so many weavers had died without passing on their knowledge. When her niece encouraged her to teach people of all walks of life, ages, and ethnicities, Lee knew it was her responsibility "to share God's gift."[76] Today, Elizabeth is credited with helping scores of individuals learn weaving. Small numbers of members of her group hold meetings throughout the year, but an annual workshop held outdoors in Kona sometimes attracts nearly two hundred haumāna from the Hawaiian Islands, as well as from Japan and the U.S. mainland, occasionally including American Indian weavers. After an opening ceremony that typically includes a prayer, a chant, and often a hula, kumu work closely with haumāna on specific lau hala projects. The nurturing environment includes constant talk story by both kumu and haumāna. Additionally, each time a student finishes a project a rousing round of applause follows. On the fourth and final day of the workshop, the learning experience is topped off by a lū'au with more music and hula, a silent auction to benefit the group, and a fashion show in which each kumu and his or her students, adorned with their completed mea ulana, parade before and are applauded by all.[77]

Not only do these groups serve to foster knowledge of weaving for their members, they also help communicate knowledge of weaving to others and help provide woven items important to the perpetuation of other cultural traditions. For instance, members of 'Aha Pūhala O Puna have spent weekends gathering and preparing the estimated 1,500 three-quarter-inch strips of lau hala needed to teach students at the Moku O Keawe festival how to make pale ipu, the square pads on which hula chanters pound their gourds.[78]

On Notions of Excellence in Weaving

Always remember your hat or whatever you weave is a reflection of yourself.[79]
Michael Nāho'op'i'i, 2005

Standards of excellence are firmly established and well known within Hawaiian lau hala weaving communities, and those with exceptional skills at weaving or teaching about it are given honor and respect as kumu, as elders, as masters.

Beginning weavers know that they must pass the scrutiny of both teachers and peers and must meet the community standards of excellence.[80] Adherence to the cultural values, norms, and beliefs—and equally important, the character of the weaver—is fundamental to community-based notions of what makes a good lau hala woven hat or object.

For many weavers, making a pāpale is more than simply creating a hand-made object; it is a form of expressing oneself culturally in a deeply felt act that has spiritual dimensions. A student of Gladys Grace reflected on this: "One of the things that Aunty Gladys always says is when you are weaving, what you feel in your heart is what happens with your hands and you can see it in the hat. So if you're feeling tired or upset, put down the lau hala and walk away. You can see the changes in your hat. If you're feeling angry and start pulling real tight, you can see it. If you want a good quality hat, you have to have a good heart and put that into your hat."[81] Excellence requires not only mastery of technique and a deep respect for cultural practices, but also having a sense of personal well-being and a rightness of the heart.

Contemporary Challenges to Lau Hala

Finding lau hala on Oʻahu is extremely difficult. . . . In the past, it was abundant on the windward coast. You have to climb mountains to get it now. Cities and counties in the state are planting lau hala, but it's next to the freeways so it gets soot from cars.[82] Gwen Mokihana Kamisugi, 2005

Despite its interconnections to and its widespread use in Hawaiian history and culture, there are contemporary challenges to the continuing presence of lau hala weaving in Hawaiʻi. Sadly, nearly all of the work available for sale in Hawaiian marketplaces is imported from other countries, and there are few places where locally made mea ulana is sold. Even more sobering is that there are few cultural tradition bearers who not only have the expert skills to weave lau hala but, more importantly, have the knowledge about locating, harvest-ing, and caring for hala trees, preparing lau for weaving, the language to de-scribe techniques and designs, and the stories, songs, dances, and chants that connect the art to the culture. As expressed by educational leader Maenette Benham, "With each passing generation of kūpuna, the ʻike of Kanaka Maoli 'national treasures' are diminishing."[83]

At one time, many lau hala weavers regularly and easily supplemented their income by making lau hala for sale even though the market price barely reflected the amount of labor it took to gather, prepare, and then weave the lau into hats and other objects. Alice Kawamoto and her daughters are one of the few families that still produce work in volume. Today the few sales outlets for the work of weavers include some museum gift shops, craft fairs, and Native Hawaiian events like the annual Merrie Monarch Festival in Hilo. A few commercial outlets bear special mention. Nā Mea Hawaiʻi/Native Books, a store in Honolulu that specializes in local Hawaiian arts and books on Hawaiian culture, is the site of regular lau hala classes and demonstrations. Nakeʻu Awai in Honolulu has been a patron of the work of lau hala weavers and has hosted fashion shows that include lau hala.[84] Kimura Lauhala Shop, established in 1914 in Hōlualoa, has long served as the key sales outlet for hats produced by weavers on Hawaiʻi Island.[85] Recently Pōhako Kahoʻohanohano has opened a store on Maui devoted to lau hala where he sells his and other artists' work. Some weavers have turned to Web sites, YouTube, blogs, and other social media tools to help promote their work and to find buyers. Cherie Okada-Carlson, for instance, provides current news about weavers, weaving organizations, and weaving events on her Web site.[86]

Another challenge to lau hala in the twenty-first century is access to the very materials upon which the weaving depends. Lau hala weavers are careful and concerned stewards of plant resources. They have a deep and abiding respect for the land and extensive knowledge of how to harvest and care for plants in order to sustain healthy growth and ensure the availability of these

Kimura Lauhala Shop, Hōlualoa, Kona, Hawaiʻi Island. Image courtesy of Marsha MacDowell.

precious resources far into the future. Yet all weavers talk of the difficulties in gaining access to good sources of lau hala, and, on Maui, an invasive insect is beginning to devastate groves of hala.[87] Stands of hala have always been treasured and cared for by Native Hawaiians. When Pōhaku was researching his family's landholdings on Maui, he discovered in early documents that a hala grove was one of the noted assets.[88] Today, many of these groves have been destroyed by human encroachment; buildings stand where hala once thrived, and existing stands are on property that is now private and rendered largely inaccessible to those weavers who want to care for hala and harvest the lau. Ironically, some hala palms grow in urban settings or alongside some roadsides, but the pollution from cars blackens and pockmarks the leaves.

Although kumu have always been respected in their communities, there has been relatively little public recognition of the tremendous contributions they have made to mastering and perpetuating the art of lau hala. However, slowly but surely, kumu are being recognized through the Hawai'i State Foundation on Culture and the Arts and the Office of Hawaiian Affairs. In 2011, the National Endowment for the Arts awarded Gladys Grace a National Heritage Fellowship Award, one of the nation's most prestigious awards for artists.

Documenting, Preserving, and Bringing New Attention to Lau Hala

In the early 2000s, a national project coordinated by the Michigan State University Museum, the National Museum of the American Indian, and the Smithsonian Center for Folklife and Cultural Heritage in collaboration with Native Hawaiian, American Indian, and Alaskan Native artists and organizations aimed to address issues of concern to indigenous weavers in the United States. Called Carriers of Culture: Living Native Basket Traditions, the initiative resulted in several gatherings of indigenous weavers to discuss needs and to plan for a special program at the 2006 Smithsonian Folklife Festival held on the National Mall in Washington, DC.

In 2005, as preparation for the event in Washington, DC, Sabra Kauka organized E Ho'omau Nā Mea Ulana Hina'i, a gathering on Kaua'i of invited weavers from all the islands.[89] At the Kaua'i gathering, weavers talked about their personal and collective experiences and then began to identify their common concerns. Carriers of Culture at the Smithsonian festival in 2006 brought together over one hundred master artists, including twelve from Hawai'i. The Hawaiian contingent demonstrated making lau hala woven pāpale, led hands-on children's activities, and participated in public discussion panels and talk story sessions. One-on-one artist-to-visitor encounters shared the making and use of woven hats. Thousands of festival visitors learned about the artistry, ceremonial and everyday use, and issues connected to lau hala weaving and pāpale within Native Hawaiian culture.

For the Smithsonian festival, the weavers from Hawai'i planned to put up a temporary display of fifty hats since the Hawaiian delegation represented the fiftieth state in the union.[90] They brought to the National Mall hats they either made themselves or had borrowed from friends and family. Almost immediately upon seeing their display they realized it was the first time that any of them had witnessed such a large exhibit of contemporary hats. Certainly they had seen small displays of historical hats in museums and had seen contemporary hats worn in churches and at events in Hawai'i, but to see so many together in one place was impressive and something to behold. The Hawaiian weavers, the other indigenous weavers participating in the festival, and the visitors to the festival responded with delight to the stunning variety of shapes, forms, and artistry of the pāpale displayed in Washington.

As a direct result of Carriers of Culture, the program curators and the Hawaiian weavers became even more acutely aware of the need to gather more documentation and to do more to bring greater attention to the importance of lau hala in contemporary Hawaiian culture.[91] Two more organizational

Weavers at the Carriers of Culture exhibit at the Smithsonian Folklife Festival, 2006. Image courtesy of Marsha MacDowell.

partners—The Bernice Pauahi Bishop Museum, followed by the Hawaiʻinuiākea School of Hawaiian Knowledge at the University of Hawaiʻi at Mānoa—joined Michigan State University Museum and the artists in an initiative called the ʻIke Pāpale project to further document, analyze, describe, and present the many rich ways that lau hala is part of Hawaiian cultural knowledge and identity. Since 2010, members of the ʻIke Pāpale project team have been gathering the stories of many makers and users of hats, documenting the use of pāpale in Hawaiian life, locating and documenting examples of pāpale and historical photographs and accounts of its use, and identifying the use of lau hala in music, song, dance, and popular culture.[92]

All the partners are committed to community-engaged research on cultural traditions and then to convey the knowledge collected in ways that will advance further scholarship, enhance the education of the public, and, importantly, help the traditional artists and knowledge bearers sustain their important work. This body of collected resources will form the largest existing collection of materials on lau hala and will reside in two repositories in Hawaiʻi (Hawaiʻinuiākea School of Hawaiian Knowledge at the University of Hawaiʻi at Mānoa, and The Bernice Pauahi Bishop Museum) and a small collection of pāpale and duplicate records on the mainland at Michigan State University Museum. To the extent it is culturally appropriate, the intention is to make these data about hats, hat makers, and hat traditions easily accessible to artists, scholars, educators, and both Hawaiians and non-Hawaiians.

The Carriers of Culture program at the Smithsonian also served as a stimulus for action on the concerns articulated by weavers in Kauaʻi and further discussed in Washington. Immediately following the DC event, several of the Hawaiian weavers arranged for an exhibition at the airport in Kauaʻi of a smaller selection of the hats shown at the Smithsonian festival. Subsequently, The Bernice Pauahi Bishop Museum mounted the exhibition *Ka Lei Pāpale: Hats of Hawaiʻi*, which drew extensively from its historical collection, much of which belonged to the museum's namesake, Princess Bernice Pauahi Bishop, and was supplemented with a number of contemporary examples. This exhibition was important in that it not only showed that hat making was a continuing, living art, but it also demonstrated that contemporary artists were both drawing on traditions and creating work that also incorporated new designs and cross-cultural influences.[93] Shortly after Gladys Grace received the National Heritage Fellowship honor, the Honolulu Museum of Art organized the exhibition *Ulana Me Ka Lokomaikaʻi: To Weave from the Goodness Within*, which showcased Gladys's hats as well as examples from many of her haumāna.[94] The exhibition beautifully demonstrated the weaving connections between kumu and haumāna. These were the first museum exhibitions to emphasize contemporary lau hala art.

Students and their pāpale at the *Ulana Me Ka Lokomaika'i* exhibit, 2011. Photo by Shuzo Uemoto, courtesy of Honolulu Museum of Art.

Last Words

There is no word in Hawaiian language for art. I see art as being a visual conversation or language to express. Some people talk in words. Some people are writers or historians—they write things down. Artists do it in a visual way and it speaks about who we are and what we're doing. . . . Being a Native Hawaiian, I choose things that speak in depth to my people and what they need to know.[95] Hāli'imaile Andrade, 2005

Lau hala weaving is a culturally important art that has, to date, been little understood by those unfamiliar with Hawaiian history and culture. To the extent that art is "a visual conversation or language," knowledge about lau hala weaving in Hawai'i is a means to understanding that Hawaiian cultural heritage. It is hoped that this book and the activities of the 'Ike Pāpale documentation project will help firmly situate knowledge about lau hala weaving and its associated cultural traditions in the written literature on Hawaiian culture and that these written words, along with the stories, mele, oli, and the ulana itself, will help advance an understanding of Hawaiian history and what it means to be Hawaiian.

NOTES

The authors wish to thank the following individuals who were especially helpful: Caroline Affonso, Ku'ulani Auld, Maenette Benham, Molly Brown, Marit Dewhurst, Gladys Grace, Barbara Harger, Pōhaku Kaho'ohanohano, Betty Kam, Gwen Mokihana Kamisugi, Ed Kaneko, Shirley Kauhaihao, Sabra Kauka, Elizabeth Maluihi Lee, Jennifer Leung, Margaret Lovett, Lynne Martin, Michael Nāho'op'i'i, Cherie Okada-Carlson, Marcia Omura, Peter Park, Deacon Ritterbush, Wesley Sen, Harriet Soong, Lola Ku'ulei Spencer, Annette Ku'uipolani Wong, Laurie Woodard, and Pearl Yee-Wong.

1. E. Kawai Aona-Ueoka, "Artist Profile," in Anne E. O'Malley, ed., *E Ho'omau Na Mea Ulana Hīna'i (A Gathering of Native Hawaiian Basketweavers)* (Lihu'e, HI: Ho'oulu Ke Ola O Na Pua, Garden Island RC&D, 2005), 10.

2. "Lau hala" is sometimes spelled as one word, "lauhala," in this chapter when it appeared that way in the citation source. Similarly, words are spelled with diacritics unless they appear otherwise in the citation source.

3. Gladys Grace quoted in C. Kurt Dewhurst, Marsha MacDowell, and Marjorie Hunt, "Carriers of Culture: Native Basketry in America," *2006 Smithsonian Folklife Festival* (Washington, DC: Smithsonian Institution Center for Folklife and Cultural Heritage, 2006), 49.

4. Entry number 2746, Mary Kawena Pukui, *'Ōlelo No'eau: Hawaiian Proverbs and Poetical Sayings* (Honolulu: Bishop Museum Press, 1997).

5. Timothy Gallaher, "The Past and Future of Hala (*Pandanus tectorius*) in Hawai'i," this volume.

6. Adren J. Bird, Steven Goldsberry, and J. Puninani Kanekoa Bird, *The Craft of Hawaiian Lauhala Weaving* (Honolulu: University of Hawai'i Press, 1982), 14.

7. Caren Loebel-Fried, *Hawaiian Legends of Dreams* (Honolulu: University of Hawai'i Press, 2005).

8. Nathaniel B. Emerson, *Pele and Hi'iaka* ('Ai Pōhaku Press, 1997), cited in Loebel-Fried, *Hawaiian Legends of Dreams.*

9. See several examples cited in Edna Williamson Stall, *The Story of Lauhala* (Hilo, HI: Petroglyph Press, 1953), 21.

10. Heidi Leianuenue Bornhorst, *Growing Native Hawaiian Plants: A How-To Guide for the Gardener* (Honolulu: Bess Press, 2005), 76. For more information on hala lei, see interview with Roy Benham in this volume as well as Marie A. McDonald and Paul R. Weissich, *Nā Lei Makamae: The Treasured Lei* (Honolulu: University of Hawai'i Press, 2003).

11. Gallaher, "Past and Future of Hala," this volume.

12. David Young, *Nā Mea Makamae: Hawaiian Treasures* (Kauila-Kona, HI: Palapala Press, 1999), 37. Olanā or semili is a type of cordage made by plaiting grasses.

13. Stall, *Story of Lauhala,* 25.

14. Makaloa (*Cyperus laevigatus* L.), also known as sedge, is a wetland plant indigenous to Hawai'i. For an excellent resource on the importance of this fiber in Hawaiian history and culture, especially on the island of Ni'ihau, see Roger G. Rose, *Patterns of Protest: A Hawaiian Mat-Weaver's Response to 19th Century Taxation and Change,* Bishop Museum Occasional Papers. Honolulu: Bishop Museum, Vol. 30 (June 1990). For a good report on a project of traditional weavers and government efforts to address diminished supplies of the plant, see Peter Van Dyke, "Growing *Makaloa (Cyperus laeviga-*

tus L.)," in *Constructed Wetlands for Weaving and Treating Wastewater. Final Report for U.S. Geological Survey Grant No. 99CRGR0003*. Bishop Museum (June 2001), http://www .bishopmuseum.org/research/pdfs/makaloa.pdf.

15. Stall, *Story of Lauhala*, 31.

16. Ibid., 33.

17. Ibid.

18. Ibid.

19. Ibid., 35.

20. Rose, *Patterns of Protest*, 88–117.

21. Ibid., 2.

22. *Ka Lahui Hawaii*, cited in Rose, *Patterns of Protest*, 112. "Pawehe" is the word used to describe the designs woven into mats, particularly on Ni'ihau, and inscribed onto gourds. See "Na Ipu o Hawai'i—the Gourds of Hawai'i," accessed May 12, 2013, http:// www.kaahelehawaii.com/pages/culture_ipu.htm.

23. See especially Rose, *Patterns of Protest*, 111–113.

24. Marcia Omura, personal communication, August 12, 2013.

25. Ibid.

26. Pōhaku Kaho'ohanohano, personal communication with Kurt Dewhurst and Marsha MacDowell, Maui Lauhala Discovery Day, Kaunoa Senior Center, Maui, Hawai'i, February 6, 2012; and Margaret Lovett, personal communication with Kurt Dewhurst, Kona, Hawai'i, May 18, 2013.

27. Stall, *Story of Lauhala*, 37.

28. According to many weavers interviewed by Marsha MacDowell and C. Kurt Dewhurst, including Edward Kaneko, Harriet Soong, Peter Park, and Elizabeth Lee, from 2004 to 2013.

29. Sabra Kauka, personal communication with Marsha MacDowell and C. Kurt Dewhurst, 2005.

30. Pōhaku Kaho'ohanohano, interviewed by Marsha MacDowell and C. Kurt Dewhurst, Oahu, Hawai'i, February 4, 2012.

31. Pōhaku Kaho'ohanohano, telephone interview by C. Kurt Dewhurst, July 29, 2013.

32. Ibid. Marcia Omura recalled the same story about Pōhaku in a communication to the authors on August 12, 2013.

33. Document files for Hawaiian Hall exhibition, Bishop Museum, Honolulu, Hawai'i, 2008–2009.

34. Maile Andrade, Eric and Barbara Dobkin Fellowship, 2012, School for Advanced Research, http://sarweb.org/index.php?artist_maile_andrade. For more examples of her work, see Maile Andrade, Native Hawaiian Visual Artist, accessed July 23, 2013, http://www.maileandrade.com.

35. Maile Andrade, interviewed by Mea Nīnauele and Melehina Groves Ka'iwakīloumoku, Makali'i, February 2006, http://apps.ksbe.edu/kaiwakiloumoku/ makalii/talking-story/maile_andrade.

36. Kaiolohia K. Funes Smith recorded Johnny Lum-Ho's "Mohala Ka Hinano" and "Puna paia 'a'ala i ka hala" on *Aloha Ku'u Home 'O Hana*, Ululoa Productions, accessed February 6, 2013, http://www.ululoa.com/site/kai.html.

37. See John Leal, "Wahine with the Lauhala Hat," accessed February 2, 2013, http://www.huapala.org/Wa/Wahine_In_Lauhala_Hat.html. This song was recorded

by Alvin Kaleolani Isaacs with the Original Royal Hawaiian Serenaders (Waikiki Records, 1998), and by Barney Isaacs on his album *E'Mau* (Aloha Records, 1995). Allmusic, accessed February 14, 2014, http://www.allmusic.com/album.emau-mw0000123322.

38. The song "Ku'u Papale Lauhala" was recorded by Leilani Bond on the album *Na Hoku O Ka Lani* (Leilani Records, 2000), and by Na Ohana Hoaloha on *Pretty Old for Our First Time*, produced by Coffees of Hawai'i, Kualapu'u, Moloka'i, 2009.

39. Kūpuna Competition, Halau Na Pua U'I O Hawaii, published on September 16, 2012, by coffeeboy5063, http://www.youtube.com/watch?v=bmuoWB+H20E.

40. Elizabeth Malu'ihi Lee, "A Song of Sharing the Lauhala," recorded and posted May 22, 2010, on YouTube by tutustromberg, http://www.youtube.com/watch?v=7YIk _VNTZWQ.

41. Michael Stein, "Sig Zane—Wearing His Culture with Pride," *Maui Magazine*, spring 2003, http://www.mauimagazine.net/Maui-Magazine/Spring-2003/Sig-Zane -Wearing-his-Culture-with-Pride/. For more information on Sig Zane, go to http://www .sigzane.com.

42. Sabra Kauka, quoted in C. Kurt Dewhurst, Marsha MacDowell, and Marjorie Hunt, "Carriers of Culture: Native Basketry in America," *2006 Smithsonian Folklife Festival* (Washington, DC: Smithsonian Institution Center for Folklife and Cultural Heritage, 2006), 55.

43. Mary Kawena Pukui, quoted in exhibition text panel, Hawai'i Hall, Bishop Museum, Honolulu, Hawai'i, 2011.

44. Exhibition files for *Ka Lei Pāpale: The Wreath of Hats,* exhibition at the Bishop Museum, Honolulu, Hawai'i, 2011.

45. Lola Ku'ulei Spencer, personal correspondence, 'Ike Pāpale Project files, Bishop Museum, Honolulu, Hawai'i, 2012.

46. Peter Park, quoted in Dewhurst, MacDowell, and Hunt, "Carriers of Culture," 58.

47. Elizabeth Maluihi Lee, "Artist Profile," in O'Malley, *E Ho'omau Na Mea Ulana Hīna'i*, 17.

48. Stall, *Story of Lauhala,* 37.

49. Ibid., 37.

50. Ibid.

51. Marcia Omura, written communication to the authors, August 12, 2013.

52. Ed Kaneko, telephone interview with C. Kurt Dewhurst, July 29, 2013.

53. Marsha MacDowell and C. Kurt Dewhurst, field notes, from attendance at multiple gatherings of Ka Ulu Lauhala O Kona, 2003–2013.

54. Document files for *Ka Lei Pāpale: The Wreath of Hats* exhibition at the Bishop Museum, Honolulu, Hawai'i, 2011.

55. Ibid.

56. Josephine Ku'uipo Kalahiki-Morales, personal communication with Marsha MacDowell, May 2005.

57. Cherie Okada-Carlson, personal e-mail communication to C. Kurt Dewhurst, March 24, 2013.

58. James Cave, "Hats of Weaves," *Honolulu Weekly*, November 28, 2012, http:// honoluluweekly.com/story-continued/2012/11/hats-of-weaves/2.

59. Marit Dewhurst, Lia O'Neill M. A. Keawe, Cherie Okada-Carlson, Marsha MacDowell, and Annette Ku'uipolani Wong, "Ka ulana 'ana i ka piko (In Weaving You

Begin at the Center: Perspectives from a Culturally Specific Approach to Art Education)," *Harvard Educational Review* (spring 2013).

60. Marcia Omura, written communication to the authors, August 12, 2013.

61. Dewhurst et al., "Ka ulana 'ana i ka piko."

62. Document files for *Ka Lei Pāpale*.

63. Marcia Omura, written communication to the authors, August 12, 2013.

64. Michael Nāhoʻopiʻi quoted in Dewhurst, MacDowell, and Hunt, "Carriers of Culture," 56.

65. *Ka Lahui Hawaii,* cited in Rose, *Patterns of Protest,* 112.

66. For her reflection of her experience of learning from kumu Gladys Grace, see Marcia Omura, "My Roots," *Bamboo Ridge: Journal of Hawaiʻi Literature and Arts* no. 81 (spring 2002).

67. Pōhaku Kahoʻohanohano, quoted in Teya Penniman, "The Weave of History," *Maui Magazine/No Ka ʻOi,* March–April 2013, http://www.mauimagazine.net/Maui -Magazine/March-April-2013/The-Weave-of-History/.

68. Cherie Okada-Carlson and Marit Dewhurst, "Becoming Haumana," *CARTS (Cultural Resources for Teachers and Students)* 12 (2011–2012): 9.

69. Michael Nāhoʻopiʻi showed us this hat he made in February 2013.

70. The Native Hawaiian Education Program for K–12 learners, the Hawaiʻinuiākea School of Hawaiian Knowledge at the University of Hawaiʻi at Mānoa, and University of Hawaiʻi at Hilo are but a few examples.

71. Lynn Martin, *Celebrating the 1977 Folk Arts Apprenticeship Gathering* (Honolulu: Honolulu Academy of the Arts, 1977). Selections of the records of this program are housed at the State Archives, Honolulu.

72. *Traditions We Share: Celebrating the 1997 Folk Arts Apprenticeship Gathering* (Honolulu: Honolulu Academy of Arts, 1997).

73. Stall, *Story of Lauhala,* 7.

74. *Honolulu Academy of Arts Bulletin* (July–August 2011): 7.

75. Flyer for Ulana Me Ka Lokomaikai Weaving Retreat, Queen Kapiolani Hotel, Honolulu, Hawaiʻi, October 7–10, 2011, https://sites.google.com/site/hawaiianlauhala.

76. Carolyn Lucas-Zenk, "Lauhala Conference Helps Perpetuate Hawaiian Art," *West Hawaii Today,* May 18, 2012, http://westhawaiitoday.com/sections/news/local -news/lauhala-conference-helps-perpetuate-hawaiian-art.html.

77. Marsha MacDowell and C. Kurt Dewhurst, field notes on Ka Ulu Lauhala O Kona, 2003–2013.

78. Catharine Lo, "The Life of the Lau," *HanaHou!* 13, no. 3 (2010): 1.

79. Michael Nāhoʻopiʻi, quoted in Dewhurst, MacDowell, and Hunt, "Carriers of Culture," 61.

80. Omura, "My Roots."

81. Michael Nāhoʻopiʻi, "Artist Profile," in O'Malley, *E Hoʻomau Na Mea Ulana Hīnaʻi,* 22.

82. Gwen Mokihana Kamisugi, quoted in Dewhurst, MacDowell, and Hunt, "Carriers of Culture," 55.

83. Maenette Benham, "ʻIke Pāpale: The Vitality and Vibrancy of Lauhala Hat Weaving Traditions in Hawaiʻi," proposal for presentation at the 2012 National Outreach Scholarship Conference, April 2012.

84. Marcia Omura, written communication to the authors, August 12, 2013.

85. Renee Kimura, interviewed by Marques Marzan, Marsha MacDowell, and Kurt Dewhurst at Kimura Store, Hōlualoa, Hawai'i, February 8, 2012. See also "Alfreida Kimura Fujita: Keeping It Personal," *Oral History Recorder* 23, no. 2 (2006): 2–7; and Betty Fullard-Leo, "Hawaiian Weaving: A Meaningful Legacy," *Coffee Times* (winter 1999), http://www.coffeetimes.com/weaving.htm.

86. Lauhalahats.com, Virtual Home of Cherie's Place and Lauhala Hats, accessed January 28, 2013, http://www.lauhalahats.com.

87. Pōhaku Kaho'ohanohano, personal communication to Kurt Dewhurst and Marsha MacDowell, February 6, 2012. Timothy Gallaher, in his chapter "The Past and Future of Hala (*Pandanus tectorius*) in Hawai'i," in this volume writes more extensively on this topic.

88. Pōhaku Kaho'ohanohano, personal communication to Marques Marzan, Kurt Dewhurst, and Marsha MacDowell, February 6, 2012.

89. O'Malley, *E Ho'omau Na Mea Ulana Hīna'i*.

90. Marcia Omura, written communication to the authors, August 12, 2013; Ed Kaneko, telephone communication with Kurt Dewhurst, August 15, 2013.

91. Hawaiian state folklorist Lynn Martin in the Nā Paniolo o Hawai'i project, one of the first major efforts to document traditional living artists and to bring attention to their work through a publication and exhibition. Through the paniolo project and Hawaiian Traditional Arts Apprenticeship Program, interviews were recorded with several lau hala weavers.

92. Activities have been supported by grants from the National Endowment for the Arts and the Institute of Museum and Library Services, with the in-kind help of many organizations and individuals, the Bishop Museum, Michigan State University Museum, and the Hawai'inuiākea School of Hawaiian Knowledge at the University of Hawai'i at Mānoa.

93. Marcia Omura, written communication with authors, August 12, 2013.

94. The exhibition was on display August 25, 2011–January 29, 2012. In conjunction with the exhibition, the museum worked with local weavers to offer many demonstrations and in-gallery, hands-on participatory activities for visitors. See "Ulana me ka lokomaika'i: To Weave from the Goodness Within," Honolulu Museum of Art, accessed July 31, 2013, http://www.honolulumuseum.org/art/exhibitions/11644-ulana_me_ka _lokomaikai_weave_goodness_within.

95. Hāli'imaile Andrade, "Artist Profile," in O'Malley, *E Ho'omau Na Mea Ulana Hīna'i*, 10.

BIBLIOGRAPHY

Abbott, Isabella Aiona. *Lā'au Hawai'i: Traditional Hawaiian Uses of Plants.* Honolulu: Bernice Pauahi Bishop Museum Press, 1992.

"Alfreida Kimura Fujita: Keeping It Personal." *Oral History Recorder* 23, no. 2 (2006): 2–7.

Bird, Adren J., Steven Goldsberry, and J. Puninani Kanekoa Bird. *The Craft of Hawaiian Lauhala Weaving.* Honolulu: University of Hawai'i Press, 1982.

Bornhorst, Heidi Leianuenue. *Growing Native Hawaiian Plants: A How-To Guide for the Gardener.* Honolulu: Bess Press, 2005.

Brigham, William T. *Mat and Basket Weaving of the Ancient Hawaiians Described and Compared with the Basketry of the Other Pacific Islanders.* Memoirs of the Bishop Museum 2(1), 1892.

Buck, Peter H. *Arts and Crafts of Hawaii.* Special Publication 45. Honolulu: Bernice Pauahi Bishop Museum Press, 1957.

Cave, James. "Hats of Weaves." *Honolulu Weekly,* November 28, 2012.

Damon, Ethel M. *Koamalu: A Story of Pioneers on Kauai, and of What They Built in That Island Garden.* 1883–1965. Honolulu: Honolulu Star Bulletin Press, 1931.

Dewhurst, C. Kurt, Marsha MacDowell, and Marjorie Hunt. "Carriers of Culture: Native Basketry in America," in *2006 Smithsonian Folklife Festival,* 46–63. Washington, DC: Smithsonian Institution Center for Folklife and Cultural Heritage, 2006.

Dewhurst, Marit, Lia O'Neill M. A. Keawe, Cherie Okada-Carlson, Marsha MacDowell, and Annette Ku'uipolani Wong. "Ka ulana 'ana i ka piko (In Weaving You Begin at the Center): Perspectives from a Culturally Specific Approach to Art Education." *Harvard Educational Review* (spring 2013).

Diamond, Heather. *American Aloha: Cultural Tourism and the Negotiation of Tradition.* Honolulu: University of Hawai'i Press, 2008.

Emerson, Nathaniel B. *Pele and Hi'iaka: A Myth from Hawai'i.* Honolulu: 'Ai Pōhaku Press, 1993.

Fullard-Leo, Betty. "Hawaiian Weaving: A Meaningful Legacy." *Coffee Times* (winter 1999). http://www.coffeetimes.com/weaving.htm.

"Ka ulana ana." *Ka Lahui Hawaii* III, no. 4 (January 25, 1877). (Translation in Hawaiian Ethnological Notes, Material Culture, Mats.) http://www.papakilodatabase.org.

Linnekin, Jocelyn S. "Defining Tradition: Variations on Hawaiian Identity, 1983." *American Ethnography,* 10(2): 241–253.

Lo, Catharine. "The Life of the Lau." *HanaHou!* 13, no. 3 (2010).

Loebel-Fried, Caren. *Hawaiian Legends of Dreams.* Honolulu: University of Hawai'i Press, 2005.

Lucas-Zenk, Carolyn. "Lauhala Conference Helps Perpetuate Hawaiian Art." *West Hawaii Today,* May 18, 2012. http://westhawaiitoday.com/sections/news/local-news/lauhala-conference-helps-perpetuate-hawaiian-art.html.

Martin, Lynn. *Celebrating the 1977 Folk Arts Apprenticeship Gathering.* Honolulu: Honolulu Academy of the Arts, 1977.

Martin, Lynn, ed. *Folklife Hawai'i: A Festival in Celebration of the 25th Anniversary of the State Foundation on Culture and the Arts, October 18–21, 1990.* Honolulu: State Foundation on Culture and the Arts, 1990.

Martin, Lynne. *Nā Paniolo o Hawai'i.* Honolulu: Honolulu Academy of Arts, 1987.

McDonald, Marie A., and Paul R. Weissich. *Nā Lei Makamae: The Treasured Lei.* Honolulu: University of Hawai'i Press, 2003.

Okada-Carlson, Cherie, and Marit Dewhurst. "Becoming Haumana." *CARTS (Cultural Resources for Teachers and Students)* 12 (2011–2012): 1, 3, 9.

O'Malley, Anne E. *E Ho'omau Na Mea Ulana Hīna'i (A Gathering of Native Hawaiian Bas-ketweavers).* Kaua'I, HI: Ho'oulu Ke Ola O Na Pua, Garden Island, 2005.

Omura, Marcia. "My Roots." *Bamboo Ridge: Journal of Hawai'i Literature and Arts* no. 81 (spring 2002).

Penniman, Teya. "The Weave of History." *Maui Magazine/Nō Ka 'Oi,* March–April 2013. http://www.mauimagazine.net/Maui-Magazine/March-April-2013/The-Weave-of -History/.

Pukui, Mary Kawena. *'Ōlelo No'eau: Hawaiian Proverbs and Poetical Sayings.* Honolulu: Bishop Museum Press, 1997.

Rose, Roger G. *Patterns of Protest: A Hawaiian Mat-Weaver's Response to 19th Century Taxation and Change.* Bishop Museum Occasional Papers 30. Honolulu: Bishop Museum, June 1990.

Stall, Edna Williamson. *The Story of Lauhala.* Hilo, HI: Petroglyph Press, 1953.

Stein, Michael. "Sig Zane—Wearing His Culture with Pride." *Maui Magazine,* spring 2003.

Van Dyke, Peter. "Growing *Makaloa (Cyperus laevigatus* L.)," in *Constructed Wetlands for Weaving and Treating Wastewater: Final Report for U.S. Geological Survey Grant No. 99CRGR0003.* Honolulu: Bishop Museum, June 2001.

Young, David. *Nā Mea Makamae: Hawaiian Treasures.* Kailua-Kona, HI: Palapala Press, 1999.

Harvesting Lau Hala in The Bernice Pauahi Bishop Museum's Photograph Collection

Betty Lou Kam

Information about lau hala can be found in so many places in Hawai'i—in the native voices of mele and oli, in the expressive storytelling of hula, in the treasured lore relating to fishing, household furnishing, and personal adornment, and in many other traditions. Data about lau hala can also be found in both text and visual documents in the collections of public and private museums, libraries, and archives throughout the islands and, indeed, around the world. One of those repositories is The Bernice Pauahi Bishop Museum's historical photograph collection of "a million images." The collection represents the work of hundreds of professional and amateur photographers and contains examples of the earliest photographic portraits made in the islands, scenes of land and sea, and documentation of ceremonial activities and daily life. Among the most interesting images are those that subtly uncover the sense of the hearts and minds of Hawai'i people. Because of the size and range of the collection, it is a resource on both continuity and change of many aspects of culture within the Hawaiian Islands. The collection is, without debate, a treasure trove where information on Hawai'i's cultural history, including the use of lau hala, can be harvested.

This chapter, based on delving into the Bishop Museum collection, provides a brief overview of the history of photography in Hawai'i, some information about noted photographers who worked in the islands, and a sampling of photographic images that provide documentation of the making of hats and the use of lau hala in Hawai'i. Themes of the development of photography in the islands and the adoption of foreign-styled hats as a part of Hawaiian attire are interwoven throughout. Finally, the chapter helps illuminate how photographs themselves, and the repositories that preserve and create access to them, are important resources for understanding cultural history.

Early Images of Hawaiian Culture

Before the advent of photography, the earliest known Western images of the Hawaiian Islands were the sketches made by John Webber, ship's artist to Captain James Cook.[1] With art he recorded forms of head covering used by Native Hawaiians. He thus documented the historical use of clothing and personal

Man of the Sandwich Islands with Feathered Helmet, Helmet Band and Cape, by John Webber, ca. 1780. While helmets were worn by Hawaiians, hats were not routinely worn in early Hawaiʻi. Photo courtesy of Bishop Museum.

Kamehameha the Great. This portrait is based on an original illustration by Louis Choris of the Russian von Kotzebue expedition. Kamehameha chose to be portrayed in Western clothing. Photo courtesy of Bishop Museum.

adornment, including helmets of gourd or feathers held together by a network of cordage worn by men on special occasions. Early Hawaiians appeared to have little other tradition of hat wearing.

On November 24, 1816, Kamehameha the Great sat for a portrait by Louis Choris, an artist for the Russian von Kotzebue expedition.[2] Kamehameha's decision to wear a red European vest for his portrait was a strong statement that Western clothing had become an acceptable part of formal attire for Hawaiian ali'i.[3]

By the time of the arrival of missionaries in Hawai'i in 1820, "Hawaiian men who associated with Europeans had acquired a taste for straw and felt hats."[4] The trend of wearing such introduced hats, with their application of both style and practicality, spread quickly among communities of Hawaiians. Hats that shielded field laborers from the blazing sun on hot and dusty plantations were a necessity, and immigrant groups who later arrived in the islands to shore up the dwindling labor force introduced more kinds of hats and head coverings.[5] In addition, Hawaiian artisans, skilled in weaving and plaiting, adapted the styles of foreign hats to the natural materials at hand, and unique, beautiful pāpale resulted. By the time photography was introduced in Hawai'i, "Hawaiian" hats were becoming a routine part of local manufacture and fashion.

Daguerreotype of David Kalākaua, 1836–1891, a young man of chiefly rank, ca. 1850, fashionably wearing a hat. On February 13, 1874, he became king of the Hawaiian Kingdom after a stormy election. Photo courtesy of Bishop Museum.

The Coming of Photography to Hawai'i

By the early 1800s, the Hawaiian Islands were attracting an increasing number of visitors. Those with faith-driven missions, ideas for financial gain, or wanderlust and adventurous spirits found the Hawaiian Islands an attractive location in which to establish new homes, missions, and places of business. The influx of new residents introduced their foreign lifestyles and ideas to Native Hawaiian communities. Honolulu and Lahaina, stopping places for reprovisioning of ships destined for other shores, were sites where tremendous cultural contact and exchange took place. A few local prominent individuals, such as Timoteo Ha'alilio,[6] traveled from Hawai'i and experienced newly conceived inventions developed in Europe and the United States. Word of these inventions and unique experiences spread throughout the islands. As the island chain became a gathering place for many and a transit stop for others, it is not surprising that discussion and demonstrations of the first example of "practical photography," the daguerreotype process, made its way to Hawaiian shores by 1845, a mere half dozen years from its introduction in Paris in 1839.[7]

This first practical photography process was difficult to master, and early daguerreotype artists in the islands established businesses with only limited success.[8] Their ventures, however, whetted the appetite of the growing number of new residents who recognized that their separation from families thousands of miles away could be made less painful with the exchange of treasured portraits. Hawai'i photography historian Lynn A. Davis uncovered an expression of this sentiment in an 1847 letter from missionary Juliette Montague Cooke to family members: "We sent you some very poor ones [photographs] taken by a Frenchman several months ago. We hesitated about sending them, fearing they would give more pain than pleasure, but as they were the best we could obtain we sent them."[9] Cooke had arrived in Honolulu with the Eighth Company of American missionaries in 1837.[10]

In later years, when single men immigrated to Hawai'i to work as plantation laborers, portrait photography had an additional purpose. The exchange of photographs between a young man in the islands with the family of an available young woman in his homeland could lead to a match and then to a "picture bride" wedding. It is common knowledge that prospective brides and grooms often sent pictures of their younger and more attractive selves rather than current photos. This often resulted in surprise and disappointment when wedding-partners-to-be met in person for the first time in Honolulu.

In 1853, German itinerant daguerreotype photographer Hugo Stangenwald and his partner Stephen Goodfellow opened their Daguerrean Gallery at the corner of Merchant and Fort Streets in Honolulu. They poetically advertised their new business with a clear call to those who had left families to establish an island residence:

Praise to the man who first employed
The orb of day, a ray of light
On a silver plate quite neat and fine
To trace the human face divine . . .

From distant lands and climes we've come
To this our far-off Island home
And many hearts do long in vain
To see their absent friends again . . .

How would they like an image true?
Reflected by the sunbeam's hue
To show your features plain and clear,
Their hours of solitude to cheer.

To send to them that precious boon
And have your picture taken soon
And quick their weeping eyes they'll wipe,
To smile on your "Daguerreotype."[11]

Stangenwald remained in business until 1857. During this time his clientele grew to include Hawaiian royalty who recognized the prestige of photographic portraits, an indication of their forward and progressive thinking. Stangenwald's portrait work, stunning in quality and beautiful in quiet aesthetics, along with his crisp outdoor landscape images, were not his only achievements. By the time he closed his business, Stangenwald had introduced other photographic processes to Hawai'i—making the art increasingly immediate and convenient.[12]

The 1860s brought innovations of relative speed and duplication in the photographic printing process when, instead of just one print, multiple prints could be made from a negative. With this innovation, the seed of commercially distributed photography was planted, and photography became available to a broader clientele, including those who had images made as well as those who collected images. The reproduction and distribution of single images also very importantly created a means to study how Hawaiian residents and their lifestyles were presented and promoted.

Reproduction of an early case photograph showing two Hawaiian women, ca. 1860. These women were likely outfitted to meet the photographer's design—stylish attire topped with hats.

Carte de visite of Hawaiian women wearing hats, ca. 1880. Photographs such as this were broadly distributed. Photo courtesy of Bishop Museum.

Photography was the first modern technological invention to sweep the world. Daguerreotypy was developed in 1838–1839, but impetus for its rapid spread was the perfection of a method by which many copies could be produced from a negative image on glass.

Concomitant with this discovery, the practice of photography shifted from the pursuit of art to the promotion of commerce. The professional photographer became the proprietor of a business that increasingly demanded quantity. The beginnings of this commercialization are to be found in the early years of daguerreotypy, but by 1860 the movement had become irresistible.[13]

With the use of glass negatives, portraits could be reprinted at will. The resulting photographic prints were more convenient and more affordable to a greater audience. Carte de visite and later cabinet photographs were two types of photograph for which multiple prints of a single image could be made and mounted on cards of a set size, and then made available for distribution.[14] Specialized storage and display albums were created for these new types of photograph formats, and the collecting of images of kings and queens, unusual landscapes, and "native" peoples became a fad that spread in Europe and the

Carte de visite of a Hawaiian girl carrying a child, both wearing hats, ca. 1880. Photo courtesy of Bishop Museum.

United States. Through the sharing of these photographic cards, individuals around the world were introduced to images of Hawaiian men, women, and children, some smartly wearing hats.

In British-influenced Hawai'i, men and women of chiefly rank quickly acquired the trappings of their aristocratic counterparts in Europe, taking up the latest fashions in clothing, living arrangements, and photography. The introduction of carte de visite photography in Hawai'i in 1862 offered opportunities to record these indications of modernity and to circulate these records far and wide. Hawaiians were no longer "the other but aristocrats to be collected as encounters with greatness."[15]

Evidence provided in the photographs in the Bishop Museum's historic collection as well as in other Hawaiian cultural heritage materials demonstrates that Hawaiian ali'i collected and often wore hats for formal portraits. Princess Bernice Pauahi Bishop owned an extensive collection of such headwear, most of which, without doubt, was made in the islands.[16] The hats in her collection display an incredible range of plaiting materials that were available and used locally in hat making.

Amateur Photographers

By the 1880s photography had grown in popularity within the islands, and the number of amateur photographers increased along with the number of professional studios, particularly in urban areas. Hawaiians and others, even in rural communities, clamored for the opportunity to have their images made. Wherever and whenever the opportunity appeared for getting portraits made, Hawaiian residents presented themselves wearing the finest clothes they could borrow or buy.[17] Their finest often included a hat with a fabric ribbon as decoration, or ornamented with a lei of leaves and flowers. Among the more prominent and affluent, the decorating of hats with "flattened" feather lei also became a favored practice and an associated symbol of status. These hat bands were based on a lei style previously made for royalty and worn either around the neck or on the head.

Of those who established studios, a few stand out because of the breadth, style, subject matter, or volume of their work. The following are some of the most significant.

Christian J. Hedemann

Christian J. Hedemann arrived in Hawai'i from Denmark with his new bride in mid-1878, newly employed as an engineer at the Hāna Plantation on the island of Maui. Neither he nor his wife spoke Hawaiian, and daily life was an interesting challenge. Meta Hedemann recounted this experience.

Carte de visite portrait of Princess Bernice Pauahi Bishop, Vienna, December 1875. Most travelers from the islands donned hats while abroad, but ease with hat-wearing quickly became part of the Hawaiian lifestyle as well. Photo by Adele, courtesy of Bishop Museum.

The Bishop Museum's collection of hats belonging to Princess Bernice Pauahi Bishop. The Bishop Museum's collection includes more than a hundred hats; thirty-nine were once owned and worn by Princess Pauahi. Photo by Dave Franzen, 2006, courtesy of Bishop Museum.

One day I remember we had a terrific shower. It came down like a big waterfall on the side of the hills. That morning the old Hawaiian man who brought milk up to our house in a little tin bucket appeared in the kitchen without a stitch of clothing on ... just as naked as the day he was born ... with the exception of wearing a hat. Water dripped from his brown body, and laughing and chatting to me he finally took off his hat to show that his pants and shirt were stuffed inside, so that when the rain stopped he would have dry clothes to put on. He was very proud over this *"nui loa maitai"* [*sic*] idea of his, but I was too taken by surprise to join in his delight.[18]

Hedemann was one of an expanding number of amateur photographers in Hawai'i. Some photographers gathered in camera clubs, sharing their experiments and knowledge of photographic processes and making arrangements for picture-taking excursions. Hedemann was an original member and the first president of the Hawaiian Camera Club, established in 1889. At the founding of the club, the *British Journal of Photography* announced the event and noted, "We learn from official sources that there are 50 amateurs in these is-

Hāna milkman, ca. 1883. The photographer's wife tells a charming story of a Hāna milkman, likely the gentleman portrayed here. Photo by C. J. Hedemann, courtesy of Bishop Museum.

"Brother and sister, both natives of the Sandwich Islands," Hāna, September 1883. Hedemann, an amateur photographer, captured images of people and scenes around Hāna that interested him. His early collection is important for its focus on rural scenes. Later, when the family moved to Honolulu, Hedemann captured images of the Honolulu Iron Works, where he was employed. Photo and caption by C. J. Hedemann, courtesy of Bishop Museum.

lands, which ought to be enough material to make the organization prosperous and useful."[19]

William Tufts Brigham

William Tufts Brigham saw the opportunity to create photographic books about Hawai'i that would contain "all that anyone here or in Europe would care to know about the Hawaiian Kingdom" and in 1889 began to collect images for the project.[20] Brigham became the Bishop Museum's first director, and though the project was never fully completed, several volumes of Memoirs of The Bernice Pauahi Bishop Museum were published under his authorship.[21] Brigham's *Mat and Basket Weaving of the Ancient Hawaiians* (Memoirs, vol. 2, no. 1, 1906) was one of the earliest published accounts of weaving in the islands. While Brigham espoused a sentiment typical of the time, namely that weaving was an art of a "lesser civilization," he also went on to articulate a respectful and nostalgic perspective: "In the whirl and rush of the twentieth century there is little time for the natural work of human hands fashioning a basket, plaiting a mat or knotting a net; the people who can only make these things as their ancestors did long generations ago are passing off the stage,

Hawaiian family with lau hala, Nāpoʻopoʻo, Hawaiʻi Island, ca. 1890. This photograph appears as the frontispiece of Brigham's *Mat and Basket Weaving of the Ancient Hawaiians.* While introduced hats quickly became part of local attire, the making of hats with lau hala caught on rapidly as well. Photo courtesy of Bishop Museum.

and the inanimate machine, the modern slave of civilized man, is doing this work,—but in how different a way!"[22]

In this volume, the author also wrote about mats and baskets from throughout the Pacific but barely mentioned the making of hats anywhere in the region. Brigham clearly recognized the decrease in mat plaiting by skilled Hawaiian hands. Mats were being replaced by other kinds of fabric and textiles created as "machine-made products." What Brigham did not make comment on was the growing art of plaiting exceptional Hawaiian hats.

Alonzo Gartley

Alonzo Gartley was a prominent businessman who settled in Hawaiʻi with his wife in 1900. Gartley became the manager of the Hawaiian Electric Company and later moved to the company of C. Brewer. In addition to his active business life, he was also a leader in civic affairs, and his contributions to the community were recognized in the naming of the University of Hawaiʻi's Gartley Hall.

During his first ten years as a resident in Hawaiʻi, Gartley was also busy as a photographer—an amateur artist whose interests led to striking images of

Hawaiian women making hats, 1903. The photographer favored scenes such as this, with these women and the hats they made. Photo by Alonzo Gartley, courtesy of Bishop Museum.

A gathering at Hōnaunau, Hawai'i Island, 1900–1910. Photo by Alonzo Gartley, courtesy of Bishop Museum.

landscapes throughout the islands. Because Gartley was also a member of the Hawai'i Promotion Committee, many of his photographs appeared in widely distributed publications sponsored by the committee. He is particularly known for his photographs of Hawaiian people in traditional activities of the day, and he was especially intrigued with photographing Hawaiian women plaiting hats.

In discussing Gartley's style of setting and capturing the portrait of the two hatmakers, art historian Lew Andrews (University of Hawai'i at Mānoa) remarks:

> It is easy to dismiss this image as an effort to record or portray a simpler, vanishing way of life on the part of someone who represented the dominant class and culture. The slightly downward angle of view can be understood as a sign of condescension. The photographer is literally looking down on his subjects. Yet the picture is also a striking portrait, remarkably forthright and engaging. The women in Gartley's images are distinct individuals and not simply specimens on display, neither are they romanticized or idealized in a self-consciously artful or painted way.[23]

Gartley's portraits of these women have intrigued many viewers, and that he chose to portray hatmakers on the island of Hawai'i is significant. While the making of mats might at that time have been in decline, the styling of Hawaiian hats was strong and the subject was attractive for this amateur photographer.

Ray Jerome Baker

When Ray Jerome Baker, a photographer from Eureka, California, first arrived in Honolulu in February 1908 with his wife Edith, he fell in love with everything Hawai'i offered. His first visit was quickly followed two years later by a return trip and a plan to permanently settle in Hawai'i. From the start, Baker was intrigued with Native Hawaiian lifestyles; he was fascinated by how people worked, played, and went about their daily lives. He found beauty in the execution of routine jobs—such as farming, fishing, and cooking. His photographs go beyond merely showing how the Hawaiians wove lau hala mats or prepared a pig for the lū'au; they capture, too, the inner pride and satisfaction of the workers. "The pictures of Ray Jerome Baker are seldom confused with those of his contemporaries who worked in Hawai'i. His approach was uniquely his own and his photographs remain unmatched in communicating the individual self-respect and spirit of the Hawaiian people."[24]

Woman making a hat of plaited lau hala ribbon, Onomea, Hawai'i Island, 1916. Photo by Ray Jerome Baker, courtesy of Bishop Museum.

Hawaiian women along the beach, Moloka'i, ca. 1924. Photo by Ray Jerome Baker, courtesy of Bishop Museum.

Hawaiian woman, ca. 1910. Photo by Ray Jerome Baker, courtesy of Bishop Museum.

Baker's images often captured a moment of action, though he occasionally was known to adjust a scene to his liking. He was interested in documenting change and, with his camera, he created photographic records of lifestyles that were rapidly vanishing. While the subject matter of Baker's work was often consistent, the moods of his images span a remarkable range. Baker continued photographing in Hawai'i, gave lectures illustrated with lantern slides, and published books.[25] At the heart of all of his endeavors was a respectful interest in the details of the culture he experienced daily.

Ray Jerome Baker continues to be regarded as one of Hawai'i's most prolific photographers; his work forms one of the Bishop Museum's most significant photographic collections.

Using a Photography Collection to Learn about Lau Hala

Collections of photographs such as those at the Bishop Museum are tremendous primary sources for studies of Hawai'i's natural and cultural history. As can be seen in the examples in this chapter, photographs provide visual data that help us understand the details of particular aspects of cultural history such as the production and use of lau hala. In sharing these images from the Bishop Museum's photographic collections, it is hoped that readers will understand the role of the museum in preserving these collections and will be encouraged to use the collections in their own research and education activities.

Interior of Dunn's Hat Shop, Fort Street, Honolulu, May 1910. Photo by L. E. Edgeworth, courtesy of Bishop Museum.

Photograph of Princess Ka'iulani holding her hat, 'Āinahau, Waikīkī, 1898. Photo by Frank Davey, courtesy of Bishop Museum.

Hawaiian group dressed for a pāʻina, Maui, ca. 1880. Photo by H. L. Chase, courtesy of Bishop Museum.

Pāʻū riders at Kapiʻolani Park, 1900–1910. Photo by Alonzo Gartley, courtesy of Bishop Museum.

Hawaiian woman with hat, ca. 1900. Photo courtesy of Bishop Museum.

Liki Ekela of Lāʻie Maloʻo, August 1937. Photo courtesy of Bishop Museum.

NOTES

1. John Webber traveled with Captain James Cook on his third voyage of Pacific discovery (1776–1780) on the *HMS Resolution.* Webber made quick sketches of views while visiting the islands, filling in details at a later time. His illustrations were then engraved for the official account of Cook's expedition, published in 1784. The Bishop Museum cares for several of Webber's original artworks.

2. Kamehameha the Great, c. 1758–1819, is heralded as the Hawai'i Island chief who united the island chain in the late eighteenth and early nineteenth centuries, thereby creating a single Hawaiian kingdom. Louis Choris visited the Pacific as draftsman on board the *Ruric,* a Russian ship sailing under the command of Lieutenant Otto von Kotzebue. Kotzebue, tasked to explore a northwest passage, visited the Hawaiian Islands and other Pacific locations, as well as the West Coast of North America in 1816.

3. Rose, *Hawaii,* 199. In November 1816, the only known portraits of Kamehameha made from life were completed by Choris. It is said that the king first sat dressed in Hawaiian dress, then changed to European clothing. Choris subsequently created several versions of the Kamehameha portrait, and this one with Kamehameha in a red vest seemed to be a favorite.

4. Wiswell, *Hawaii in 1819,* 61.

5. The Hawaiian population was decimated by foreign disease during the 1800s. In order to support agricultural ventures, Hawaiian rulers sought to bring in other ethnic groups to work on plantations. Immigrants from Asia, Europe, and even other parts of the Pacific migrated to the islands. Each group brought ethnic traditions and preferences that included favored food, recreation, clothing, and language.

6. Timoteo Ha'alilio, 1808–1844, was an early Native Hawaiian convert to Christianity and learned to read and write in English. In 1842 he traveled to Washington, DC, London, and Paris to learn about conditions and practices in other countries. Unfortunately, he died on board ship during his return trip to Hawai'i. What survived Ha'alilio was his 1843 daguerreotype portrait, made in Paris, still kept at the Hawaiian Mission Children's Society Library.

7. The term "practical photography" refers to photographic processes and styles that could be practiced and mastered by the layman. The daguerreotype, a complex process, was introduced by Louis Daguerre in Paris in 1839. This first photographic process caught on quickly even though this means of recording and fixing the image was difficult and often dangerous. The daguerreotype process produced a single image on a silver-coated copper plate. The plate was sensitized to light with silver iodide. Exposure time was usually long and initially photograph subjects were inanimate objects. Later improvements decreased the exposure time, yet people who sat for daguerreotype portraits were required to remain still and rarely smiled. The finished image was fragile to the touch, and thus was usually presented in a protective case. These images are often called case photographs.

8. Photograph historian Lynn Davis identified the earliest daguerreotype photographers in Hawai'i, Theophilu Metcalf (1845) and Senor Le Bleu (1847), but their tenures as such were short-lived.

9. Davis, *Photographers in the Hawaiian Islands,* 13.

10. "Companies" or groups of missionaries sponsored by the American Board of Commissioners for Foreign Missions were sent to the islands for missionary work.

The first company arrived from Boston in 1820. The Eighth Company came to Hawaiʻi in 1837. In all, twelve companies are recorded from 1820 through 1848.

11. Abramson, *Photographers of Old Hawaii*, 16.

12. Stangenwald is credited with introducing to Hawaiʻi the ambrotype, a positive image on glass made viewable with a dark backing, and early wet-plate negatives from which paper images were printed.

13. Darrah, *Cartes-de-visite in Nineteenth Century Photography*, 1.

14. Carte de visite and cabinet photographs were names applied to nineteenth-century formats of cards upon which thin photographs, usually albumen prints, were mounted. Cartes de visite, the earlier format, usually measured 2.5×4 inches. Cabinet photographs were larger—4.25×6.5 inches.

15. Kaeppler, "Encounters with Greatness," 259.

16. Bernice Pauahi Bishop, 1831–1884, was the last direct descendant of the Kamehameha lineage, the great-granddaughter of Kamehameha the Great. The Bernice Pauahi Bishop Museum was established by her husband, Charles Reed Bishop, to honor her.

17. Davis, *Na Paʻi Kiʻi*, 55.

18. Meta M. Hedemann, from 1878 privately printed, n.d., 15.

19. Davis, *Photographer in the Kingdom*, 90.

20. Davis, *Na Paʻi Kiʻi*, 3.

21. William Tufts Brigham, 1841–1926, was a Harvard scholar and scientist who became director in 1892. Though controversial in some regards, he worked tirelessly to develop the museum's collections and earn prestige for the institution.

22. Brigham, *Mat and Basket Weaving of the Ancient Hawaiians*, 1.

23. Andrews, "'Fine Island Views,'" 224.

24. Ronck, *Hawaiian Yesterdays*, 11.

25. Lantern slides were the predecessor of 35 mm film slides. Images were captured on glass and made viewable to audiences with the use of a large projector, originally lit with a lantern. This form of projected image was first introduced in 1849, and its use continued into the twentieth century.

BIBLIOGRAPHY

Abramson, Joan. *Photographers of Old Hawaii*. Honolulu: Island Heritage Limited, 1981.

Andrews, Lew. "'Fine Island Views': The Photography of Alonzo Gartley." *History of Photography* 25, no. 3 (2001): 219–235.

Brigham, William T. *Mat and Basket Weaving of the Ancient Hawaiians*. Memoirs of The Bernice Pauahi Bishop Museum, vol. 2, no. 1. Honolulu: Bishop Museum Press, 1906.

Darrah, William C. *Cartes-de-visite in Nineteenth Century Photography*. Gettysburg, PA: W. C. Darrah, 1981.

Davis, Lynn. *Na Paʻi Kiʻi. The Photographers in the Hawaiian Islands, 1845–1900*. Bishop Museum Special Publication 69. Honolulu: Bishop Museum Press, 1980.

Davis, Lynn Ann. *A Photographer in the Kingdom: Christian J. Hedemann's Early Images of Hawaiʻi*. Honolulu: Bishop Museum Press, 1988.

Kaeppler, Adrienne L. "Encounters with Greatness." *History of Photography* 25, no. 3 (2001).

Newhall, Beaumont. *The History of Photography.* New York: Museum of Modern Art, 1982.

Ronck, Ron. *Hawaiian Yesterdays: Historical Photographs by Ray Jerome Baker.* Honolulu: Mutual, 1982.

Rose, Roger E. *Hawaii: The Royal Isles.* Honolulu: Bishop Museum Press, 1980.

Wiswell, Ella. *Hawaii in 1819: A Narrative Account by Louis Claude de Saulses de Freycinet.* Notes and Comments by Marion Kelly. Pacific Anthropological Record 26. Honolulu: Bishop Museum Press, 1978.

He Momi Waiwai Ko Kākou Mau Kūpuna

Annette Kuʻuipolani Wong

ʻAʻohe wāwae o ka iʻa. ʻO ʻoe ka mea wāwae, e kiʻi mai. (Pukui, 1983)

This chapter explores the life of Elizabeth Maluihi Lee, a living treasure and master lau hala weaver from Kona, Hawaiʻi. She tells how she has continued to share her knowledge of the art of lau hala weaving with the community throughout her life. As the founder and president of the Ka Ulu Lauhala o Kona weaving organization, she explains how its annual conference was established and how this event has welcomed other master weavers to share their knowledge of lau hala weaving with the community to perpetuate this art form for current and future generations. The author also discusses the different styles of piko that Aunty Maluihi uses in weaving a pāpale lau hala and that of her own grandfather, Ernest Enoka Kaʻohelauliʻi, a master lau hala weaver from Puʻuwai Niʻihau. Aunty Maluihi also shares her wisdom about the proper way of wearing pāpale lau hala with adornments.

ʻO kēia wahi ʻōlelo noʻeau e kau maila ma luna nei, he ʻōlelo ia e aʻo mai ana iā kākou na kākou e kiʻi i ka ʻike. Aia nō ka loaʻa mai o ka ʻike iā kākou ke hele kākou e kiʻi. Ua koho ʻia kēia ʻōlelo noʻeau ma muli hoʻi o koʻu hele ʻana i mua o kekahi kupuna a nīele i kona aʻo ʻana mai i ka ʻike no ka ulana lau hala. He momi waiwai ko kākou mau kūpuna a he momi laha ʻole kekahi. Ua mano-mano ka ʻike o nā kūpuna a he ʻike hoʻi ia a lākou i aʻo maoli ai mai ko lākou mau mākua a pau pū me nā kūpuna kekahi. Ua kū hoʻi kēia ʻōlelo noʻeau aʻu i koho iho nei i kaʻu hana ma ka hele ʻana i mua o ke kupuna a nīele i kona ʻike. No ka mea, ʻo ka poʻe i lawe a mālama i ka ʻike o nā mākua a kūpuna, ʻo lākou ke pōmaikaʻi mau. ʻO kekahi, ʻo kēia ʻano aʻo makua, he ʻike ia e paʻa loa ai ma ka papa o ka naʻau o ke keiki. A he mea ʻike maka a lohe pepeiao hoʻi kēia naʻu i ka hana a me ka ʻōlelo i lohe pepeiao ʻia mai kēia wahi kupuna makamae a kaulana hoʻi ʻo ia i ka ulana lau hala ʻoia hoʻi ʻo Kupuna Elizabeth Maluihi Lee. I koʻu wā i nīele ai iā ia na wai i aʻo iā ia i ka hana no ka ulana lau hala, ua haʻi maila ʻo ia na kona makuahine hānai nō i aʻo iā ia i ka hana no ka ulana lau hala. Hele pū ʻo ia me ia a kiʻi i nā lau hala a hoʻomaʻemaʻe, a ma hope o ia hana, ulana i ka pāpale lau hala. ʻAʻole ʻo ia i haʻalele i ia ʻike ulana lau hala a hiki i kēia manawa. 'O kekahi mea e 'ike 'ia ai ka 'oia'i'o o nei 'ōlelo, ma kona mālama 'ana i kekahi 'aha ulana lau hala i kapa 'ia 'o Ka Ulu Lauhala o Kona.

Ko'u Launa 'ana me Kupuna Elizabeth Maluihi Lee

I ko'u hui mua 'ana a launa pū me kupuna Elizabeth Maluihi Lee, ma ka 'Aha Mānaleo mua loa i mālama 'ia ma ka hōkele 'o Prince i Waikīkī i mau maka-hiki i ka'a hope aku nei. Ma ia hui pū 'ana o māua au i 'ike ai i kona 'ohu'ohu 'ana i kona po'o i ka pāpale lau hala. I ko'u 'ike 'ana iā ia i ka 'ohu'ohu i ka pāpale lau hala, he nani ho'i kau ke nānā aku a ho'omana'o ihola au i ko'u kupunakāne. He kanaka 'ohu'ohu mau 'o ia i ka pāpale lau hala. 'A'ole nō ho'i 'o Kupuna Lee wale nō ka'u i 'ike ai i ka 'ohu'ohu 'ia i ka pāpale lau hala ma ia 'aha mānaleo, he mau kūpuna hou aku nō kekahi. A 'o Kupuna Maluihi Lee, 'oia ho'i ka inoa i ho'olauna 'ia ia'u, 'a'ohe wā a'u i 'ike ai i kona po'o i ka hele lākā wale iho nō 'a'ohe pāpale lau hala. 'Ohu'ohu mau 'ia kona po'o i kēlā me kēia wā i ka pāpale lau hala a 'ohu'ohu pū 'ia kona pāpale lau hala i ka lei hulu kekahi. Iā Kupuna Maluihi Lee nō au i lohe mua ai i kēia 'ōlelo, mai komo wale nō i ka pāpale lau hala me ka 'ohu'ohu 'ole 'ia o ka pāpale i ka lei. 'O ka lei e 'ohu'ohu ai i ka pāpale lau hala, aia nō i ka mea nāna e 'ohu'ohu ana. 'O ka mea ma'a mau ho'i a'u i 'ike ai, 'o ia ho'i ka lei hulu. 'O ko'u Kupunakāne na'e, he nui nā 'ano lei āna i 'ohu'ohu ai i kona pāpale lau hala. 'O ka lei hulu kolohala 'oe, ka lei hulu pīkake 'oe, ka lei 'ano'ano koa haole 'oe, ka lei wiliwili 'oe, a 'o ka lei pūpū 'ōlepe Ni'ihau nō ho'i kekahi. Ua 'ohu'ohu 'o ia i nā lei hulu a me ka lei pūpū 'ōlepe ma kona pāpale no ka hele 'ana i ka pule. 'O ke kumu no kona 'ohu'ohu 'ana i kēia 'ano kaila lei no ka pāpale, no kona u'i. 'O ka lei hulu manu pīkake a me ka manu hulu kolohala, he mau lei u'i nō ke nānā aku. 'O kekahi, aia nō i ke kaila i humu papa 'ia. 'O ka lei hulu pīkake, humu papa 'ia nā hulu o ka 'ā'ī o ka manu pīkake. A pēlā nō me nā hulu manu kolohala. Humu papa 'ia nā hulu mai ka 'ā'ī o ke kolohala. A 'o ia paha ke kumu i lei 'ia ai ka pāpale lau hala i ka lei hulu ma muli o kona u'i. Ua like nō me nā lole i 'a'ahu 'ia ma nā Lāpule. Ua komo 'ia nā lole nani e nā wāhine e la'a ho'i me ka mu'umu'u 'oe, ka holokū 'oe a pēlā wale aku. 'O kēia 'ano kaila lole, he mau lole nō ia i 'a'ahu 'ia no ka hele wale 'ana nō i ka pule. 'O kekahi, ma ka lole 'oe e 'ike ai i ko kūlana o ke kanaka a e hō'ike mai ana iā kākou, he lā hele pule nō ia. 'O nā lole 'ālaulau, ua komo wale 'ia nō i ka lā hālāwai noa a i 'ole no ka holoholo kauhale 'ana. 'O ia kekahi mea e hō'ike ai i ke kanaka he lole hele pule a i 'ole he lole hele hālāwai noa a holoholo kauhale nō ho'i ia. A pēlā nō ke komo 'ana i ka lei pūpū a me nā 'ano lei i 'ohu'ohu 'ia ma ka pāpale kekahi. O nā lei 'ano'ano, ho'ohana wale 'ia nō no ka hele 'ana i ka holoholo kau hale a i 'ole i ka lā hālāwai 'ohana. 'A'ole nō ko'u kupunakāne i 'ohu'ohu i ka lei 'ano'ano ma ka pāpale no ka hele 'ana i ka pule. Ua lei wale 'ia nō ma ka 'ā'ī. Eia na'e, kāka'ikahi ko lākou lei 'ana i ka lei ʻanoʻano wiliwili. Ke manaʻo nei au, mamuli paha o ke kaumaha o ia ʻano lei ʻanoʻano ke lei ʻia ma ka pāpale. ʻO ka lei ʻanoʻano wiliwili, kaumaha nō kona ʻano. Ke kuhi nei au, ma muli o kona kaumaha, he mea ia e hoʻowela ai i ke poʻo kekahi. ʻO kekahi, ke hele a maneʻo a i ʻole wela ke poʻo, ʻaʻole make-make ka mea pāpale i ka pāpale e wehe i kona pāpale i loko o ka halepule o ʻike ʻia auaneʻi ka pūkalakī o ka lauoho. No ka mea, ke wela ke poʻo a wehe ʻia ka pāpale, pīpili ka lauoho ma ka pāpale. A i ʻole ia, hoʻomāka ʻia ka lauoho e ka pāpale. A ʻo ia nō paha kekahi kumu i wehe ʻole ai nā kūpuna ʻohuʻohu pāpale i ka pāpale ma ka Lāpule. No ka pāpale ʻana i ka lā hālāwai a i ʻole ka holoholo ʻana paha, hiki nō ke wehe wale ʻia ka pāpale i nā ʻano wā like ʻole. Ma Niʻihau, no ka hele ʻana i ka pule i ka Lāpule a me ka lā hālāwai noa, aia nō ka pule ma ka halepule ʻo Iubile. Eia naʻe, ua wehe nā kānaka hana i ko lākou pāpale kapu i ka lā pule hālāwai noa i loko o ka halepule. ʻO kekahi mea nāna i hoʻokāhāhā i koʻu noʻonoʻo i ke kumu i wehe ʻole ai nā kūpuna i ko lākou pāpale lau hala i loko o ka halepule i ka Lāpule, maliʻa ua like nō ke kūlana o ka pāpale lau hala me ke kūlana o ka lole a lākou i ʻaʻahu ai no ka hele ʻana i ka Lāpule. No ka poʻe pāpale i ka pāpale lau hala, ʻaʻole lākou i wehe i ko lākou pāpale i loko o ka halepule. Ua kau ka pāpale i ke poʻo mai ka hiki ʻana i ka halepule a hoʻokuʻu ka pule. Nui nō nā poʻe kūpuna i ʻohuʻohu i nā pāpale lau hala no ka hele ʻana i ka pule.

Ka Lei Hulu

ʻO ka lei hulu, he nui nō nā ʻano lei hulu i ʻohuʻohu ʻia i ka pāpale lau hala. ʻO ka poʻe Niʻihau naʻe, na lākou nō i humu papa i ko lākou lei hulu ponoʻī. Ua ʻohiʻohi ʻia nā hulu kolohala a me nā hulu manu pīkake i heleleʻi a humuhumu ʻia i lei hulu. Ua ʻike nō hoʻi au i kēia hana he humu papa mai koʻu Kupuna wahine mai ʻo Ponikani. Kapa aku au iā ia ʻo tūtū Poni. He wahine pākela ʻo ia ma ka humu papa ʻana i ka lei hulu no ka pāpale lau hala a koʻu Kupunakāne i ʻohuʻohu ai. Ma ka nānā wale aku nō i ka nani o nā lei hulu i humu papa ʻia, he hoʻohihi hoʻi kau. Ua ʻike maka au i kekahi o nā lei hulu āna i humu papa ai a aia nō ia mau lei hulu i koʻu makuahine kahi e mālama ai. He ʻelua lei hulu, hoʻokahi lei hulu kolohala a hoʻokahi lei hulu pīkake. He nani maoli nō kāna mau lei hulu i humu papa ai a ʻaʻohe lua e like ai. ʻO ka mea minamina naʻe o kēia ʻike humu papa lei hulu ona, ʻaʻole kekahi o kāna mau moʻopuna i naku aku e aʻo mai i ka humu papa i kona wā e ola ana. Noʻu iho, he mea nui ke aʻo ʻana mai i ia ʻano hana ʻo ka humu papa lei hulu i wahi e ʻike ʻia ai he ʻike humu papa nō kā ko ka poʻe Niʻihau.

Ua like nō hoi ia hana me koʻu aʻo ʻole ʻana i ka ulana lau hala. ʻAʻole au i aʻo mai i ia ʻike ulana lau hala o koʻu kupunakāne. I ia wā, he kamaliʻi wale ana nō au. ʻAʻole nō i komo mai ka hoihoi ulana lau hala i loko oʻu i ia wā. Akā, i ka hele 'ana a lilo maila i kanaka makua, komo maila ka hoihoi i loko o'u no nei hana ulana pāpale lau hala. A kūnānā ka maka iā ha'i no ka mea, ua ho'i ko'u kupunakāne i ke ala ho'i 'ole mai 'o ia ho'i ke ao iā Kāloa mā. Pono nō au e 'imi i kēia 'ike maiā ha'i mai kekahi kanaka pili koko 'ole ia'u. Minamina nō ho'i ke no'ono'o a'e i ia wā e ola ana 'o nā kūpuna a 'a'ole i komo mai ka hoihoi i loko o'u e noho pū me ia a a'o mai i ka hana no ka ulana lau hala. I pololei wale ai ka 'ōlelo kaulana a nā kūpuna i haku ai i loko o ke mele o "Nā 'Ono o ka 'Āina." "Mai kali a pau nā niho, o hala e ka pu'ulena." He ha'awina ho'i kēia e a'o mai ana ia'u a iā kākou ho'i a pau ka po'e e heluhelu mai ana i kēia wahi mana'o a'u e kākau nei i mua o 'oukou. Inā loa'a kekahi kupuna ou me ia 'ike, e a'o mai i kona 'ike i kona wā e ola mai ana. 'O ia ka wā e a'o ai a pa'a ko lākou 'ike ma ka papa o ka na'au. Mai kali a pau nā niho o kū 'oe i ka 'ōlelo o kēia mele. Ma 'ane'i ua kō maila ka 'ōlelo no'eau i hō'ike 'ia ma luna a'e nei, 'A'ohe wāwae o ka i'a. 'O 'oe ka mea me ka wāwae, e ki'i aku i ka i'a. 'O wau ho'i ka mea me ka wāwae e ki'i aku ai i ka 'ike ulana lau hala o nei kupuna a a'o mai i ua 'ike ala mai ka po'e e ho'omau nei i ka 'ike o ko lākou mau kūpuna.

Nā Loea Ulana Lau Hala

He mahalo palena 'ole ko'u i nā kūpuna e ho'omau nei i ia hana no'eau ulana lau hala. Iā Anakē Gladys Kukana Grace, 'o Kupuna Elizabeth Maluihi Lee, a 'o Minnie Kaawaloa. Inā nō paha 'a'ole lākou nei i ho'omau a ho'omanawanui i ka ho'ōla i kēia 'ike ulana lau hala, 'a'ole nō paha i ola kēia 'ike a hiki i kēia au iā kākou e holo nei. A he mau kūpuna ulana lau hala hou aku nō paha ma waho a'e o lākou i ho'omau i kēia 'ike ma 'ō a ma 'ane'i o ka pae 'āina 'o Hawai'i nei, no lākou pū kekahi kēia leo mahalo no ka ho'omau 'ana i ka hana ulana lau hala. Ma muli wale nō o ko lākou ho'omau 'ana i kēia hana, ua ola kēia 'ike ulana lau hala a hiki i kēia au e holo nei. 'Oiai, 'oko'a kahi a lākou i noho ai, eia na'e, 'o ka hana, ua like nō.

Ka Ulana 'ana i ka Pāpale Lau Hala

'O kēia hana he ulana pāpale lau hala, 'a'ole nō la he hana li'ili'i, he hana nui nō inā 'akahi nō 'oe a komo i loko o kēia hana he ulana lau hala. Ho'omana'o a'ela au i ko'u 'ike mua 'ana iā Kupuna Elizabeth Maluihi Lee i ka ulana pāpale lau hala. Ia'u ho'i i hō'ā aku ai i ke kīwī no ka nānā 'ana i ka papahana 'o Mānaleo, ua 'ike akula au 'o ia kā ka hoakipa o ia ahiahi. Ma ka ho'omaka 'ana o ia polo-kalamu, ua hō'ike 'ia maila 'o Kupuna Maluihi Lee e ulana ana i ka pāpale lau hala. I ia wā koke iho nō, kau maila ka hāli'ali'a ma luna o'u no ko'u Kupunakāne, 'o Enoka Ka'ohelauli'i. He kanaka ulana pāpale lau hala 'o ia i kona wā e ola ana ma Ni'ihau. I ko'u nānā 'ana iā Kupuna Maluihi Lee i ka ulana i kāna pāpale lau hala, he hana nui ke nānā aku ma muli wale nō o nā lau makaliʻi i hoʻohana ʻia no ka ulana ʻana i ka pāpale. ʻO kekahi, hele a huikau koʻu maka i ka nui hewahewa o nā lau hala i hoʻohana ʻia i ka wā hoʻokahi. Ua piʻi maila ka pīhoihoi i loko o koʻu naʻau i ka ʻike aku i ka ʻeleu maoli nō o ka manamana lima o Kupuna Maluihi Lee i ke kiʻi ʻana i nā lau hala a ulana. Noʻonoʻo ana au i loko iho oʻu ē, pehea lā! Iā Kupuna Maluihi Lee hoʻi e kamaʻilio ana me Kalani Akana, ʻaʻole nō kona maka i nānā i ka hana a kona mau lima. ʻO ka wikiwiki o ka waha i ka walaʻau, pēlā nō ka wikiwiki o kona mau lima kekahi ma ka ulana ʻana i ka lau hala. ʻO kēia ka mea nānā i hoʻopiʻi i ka hoihoi i loko oʻu a komo pū maila ka pīhoihoi i koʻu naʻau i ka hana a Kupuna Maluihi Lee a me kona nānā ʻole ʻana i kahi a kona mau lima i kiʻi aku ai i ka lau a ulana. I ka paʻa ʻana o ka pāpale i ka ulana ʻia, he nani hoʻi kau. Hele nō hoʻi a like a like ka moe ʻana o ka lau a me ka ulana ʻana i ka pāpale. ʻAʻohe hakahaka a mākāloaloa paha. ʻAʻole ʻakahi! He like wale nō ka moe ʻana o kēlā me kēia lau hala a nani hoʻi kau ke pāpale ʻo ia i kona poʻo. Ma laila hoʻi au i ʻike ai, ua paʻa ʻiʻo nō iā ia ka ʻike ulana lau hala a kona mau mākua hānai i aʻo ai iā ia. Ma ka hopena o kāna hana, ua nani wale nō.

ʻO kekahi kumu no kēia nīnau ʻana iā Kupuna Maluihi Lee, ua makemake au e nīele iā ia i kona aʻo ʻana mai i ka ulana lau hala. Ma mua naʻe o ka hiki ʻana mai o ia wā e ninaninau aku ai iā ia, pono nō ka loaʻa ʻana o kekahi mau nīnau e nīele aku ai iā ia. Eia aʻe nō nā nīnau aʻu i manaʻo ai no ka nīele ʻana iā ia. No ke aha ʻo ia i hoʻomau ai i ka ulana lau hala? He aha nā mea e pono ai no ka ulana lau hala? Ma hea ʻo ia i ʻohi ai i nā lau hala? He aha ke ʻano o ka lau hala e ʻohi ai? Pehea e hoʻomaʻemaʻe ʻia ai ka lau? He aha nā mea e pono ai no ka hoʻomaʻemaʻe ʻana i ka lau hala? I loko o kēia mau nīnau, e nīnau pū ʻia ka mea nānā i aʻo iā ia kekahi. Pehea ʻo ia i aʻo ʻia ai? Ma ka nānā wale ʻana nō o ka maka a aʻo mai o ia ʻike? A i ʻole ma ke komo pū ʻana i loko o ka hana a i ʻole he hoʻolohe wale nō paha a aʻo mai ke keiki i ka ʻike. He mea nui ka maopopo ʻana iā kākou e pehea lā lākou i aʻo ai i kēlā mau ʻike.

Ma Niʻihau naʻe, ua noho pū ke keiki me ke kupuna a i ʻole ka makua a komo pū i loko o ka hana. ʻAʻole ʻae ʻia ka noho wale ʻana nō o nā keiki a nānā i ka hana a ka makua a i ʻole ke kupuna. Ua hoʻomaka ʻia ke aʻo ʻana i nā keiki mai ka wā kamaliʻi mai nō. Pēlā nō koʻu aʻo ʻana mai i ka hana no ka lei pūpū Niʻihau. Hele koʻu makuahine i kahakai e ʻohi ai i nā pūpū, hele pū māua ʻo koʻu kaikuaʻana kekahi. I ka wā a koʻu makuahine e kolo ai ma ka lihi ʻili e ʻohi ai i nā pūpū, ʻo māua pū kekahi me ia. Me ia aku me ia aku, ua maopopo maila iā maua ka ʻohi ʻana i nā pūpū. He nui nō nā ʻano hana like ʻole o kauhale i aʻo ʻia i ke keiki ma o ke komo pū ʻana i loko o ka hana me ka makua. ʻAʻole ʻo ka hana pūpū wale nō. ʻO ke kumu i hoʻomau ʻia ai ka hana no ka lei pūpū, ʻo ia kekahi mea e loaʻa mai ai ke kālā i ka poʻe Niʻihau. He mea ia e pono ai ka noho ʻana no ka poʻe Niʻihau e like hoʻi me Kupuna Maluihi Lee. Ua hoʻomau ʻo ia i ka hana ulana lau hala no ka mea, ʻo ia nō kekahi kumu e loaʻa mai ai ke kālā e pono ai kona noho ʻana. Inā nō paha ʻaʻole ia he mea hana kālā, ua pau paha ia ʻike i ka hoʻopoina ʻia. Manaʻo au, ua like nō ke ʻano o ke aʻo ʻana o ko Niʻihau a me ko Kona. ʻO ka mea ʻokoʻa wale nō ma waena o nā mea ʻelua, ka leipūpū a me ka lau hala. ʻO ke kanaka Niʻihau wale nō aʻu i ʻike a maopopo i ka ulana lau hala, ʻo koʻu kupunakāne. ʻO kekahi, ʻaʻole nō kaulana ka lau hala ma Niʻihau e like me ko waho nei. ʻO kekahi, ʻaʻole nō nui ka loaʻa ʻana o ka lau hala ma Niʻihau e like me ka makaloa. Nui ka poʻe ulana makaloa a kaulana ʻo Niʻihau i ka makaloa i ka wā ma mua. Eia naʻe, i ka make ʻana o ka makaloa ma muli o ka ʻai ʻia ʻana e nā holoholona i lawe ʻia a hoʻolaha ma Niʻihau, make pū ka ʻike ulana makaloa kekahi. A ʻo kekahi kumu paha i hoʻomau ʻole ʻia ai ka ulana lau hala ma Niʻihau no ka lawa ʻole o ke kumu lau hala e ulu ana ma laila. He kākaʻikahi wale nō nā kumu lau hala ma Niʻihau. Wahi a koʻu makuahine ʻo Mililani Kanahele, he ʻehā wale nō kumu lau hala i ulu ma Niʻihau. A ʻo ka mea wale nō i maopopo iā ia, ua hoʻohana ʻia kona aʻa no ka lāʻau lapaʻau ʻapu hala. Ma waho aʻe o kēlā, ʻaʻole nō ka poʻe Niʻihau i hoʻohana i ka lau hala koe naʻe koʻu kupunakāne. ʻO koʻu kupunakāne, ʻo ia wale nō ke kanaka i maopopo iaʻu, hoʻohana ʻo ia i ke aʻa hala no ka lāʻau lapaʻau ʻapu hala. Maliʻa no kona hoʻohana ʻana i ke aʻa hala, a kiʻi wale aku ʻo ia i ka lau o ka hala a ulana i pāpale. ʻO ka pāpale wale nō ka mea āna i ulana ai. ʻAʻole ʻo ia i ulana i ka moena. Ke kuhi nei au, ʻo ke kumu no kona ulana ʻole ʻana i ka moena lau hala, ʻaʻole lawa ka nui o nā lau e ulana ai a paʻa ka moena. ʻO ka makaloa wale nō kaʻu i ʻike ai i ulana ʻia i moena. ʻAʻole nō i nui nā pāpale lau hala āna i ulana ai mai ia mau kumu hala mai o Niʻihau. ʻO ka nui o nā lau hala āna i hoʻohana ai no Kauaʻi. I kona wā i kipa ai iā Kauaʻi, ua ʻohi ʻo ia i nā lau hala a hoʻihoʻi i Niʻihau. Wahi a koʻu makuahine, ʻo ka lau hala ma Niʻihau, pokopoko. ʻAʻole nō like me ka lau hala o waho nei, loloa. A ʻo ia paha ke kumu no ka ʻohi ʻana o koʻu kupunakāne i nā lau hala o Kauaʻi no ka loloa. Mahalo au i ka ʻae ʻana mai o Kupuna Maluihi Lee e nīele iā ia i kēia hana he ulana lau hala no ka mea, ʻo ia nō kekahi o nā kūpuna e hoʻomau nei i kēia ʻike ulana lau hala a hiki i kēia manawa. Maliʻa ma hope o ka nīnau ʻana iā ʻAnakē Maluihi i kēia mau nīnau, hiki nō ke nānā pū ʻia ka like a me ka ʻokoʻa inā he ʻokoʻa paha ke aʻo ʻana i nā ʻike kupuna mai kahi pae a kahi pae. Ua lohe au, no Kona Hawaiʻi mai ʻo ia a he ʻokoʻa ka ulana ʻana a ka poʻe o Kona mai ka poʻe ulana mai o kekahi pae ʻāina. He nani ia, no ka mea, ʻo koʻu kupunakāne, ua ulana ʻo ia i ka pāpale lau hala kekahi. A ʻo ke ʻano o ke kaila ulana, ua ʻokoʻa nō. Ma Kona, lohe au he ʻewalu piko i loko o ka pāpale hoʻokahi a he kaila Kona nō ia. Ua ʻike maka nō au i ia ʻano kaila Kona. Eia aʻe nō kekahi kiʻi e ʻike maka ai i ka piko o ka pāpale o Kona. He ʻewalu piko nō.

Eia aʻe no kekahi kiʻi o ka pāpale lau hala a koʻu kupunakāne i ulana ai me hoʻokahi wale nō piko.

'O ke 'ano o ka piko o kā 'Anakē Maluihi pāpale. Ho'olako 'ia ke ki'i e Annette Ku'uipolani Wong.

'O ke 'ano o ka piko a ko ka mea kākau kupuna kāne. Ho'olako 'ia ke ki'i e Annette Ku'uipolani Wong.

Mahalo na'e au i ka mālama 'ana o ko'u kaikua'ana i nei pāpale a ko'u kupunakāne a loa'a akula kekahi ki'i o ka pāpale a ko'u kupunakāne i ulana ai me ia piko ho'okahi. No laila ke pa'a mai ka 'ike ulana pāpale lau hala ia'u, hiki nō ia'u ke nānā a ho'opili i kēia 'ano kaila ho'okahi piko no ka ho'ōla hou 'ana i kēia 'ano kaila pāpale a ko'u kupunakāne i ulana ai. 'O wau wale nō i loko o ko'u 'ohana ka mea e 'i'ini nei e a'o mai i ka 'ike kupuna. 'O ka hapa nui o ko'u 'ohana, 'a'ole pipili wale mai i kēia 'ano hana he ulana lau hala. 'O ka mea min-amina na'e, 'a'ole au i nīele aku iā ia i kēia 'ike ulana lau hala i kona wā e ola mai ana. Ke ho'ohuoi nei au, mali'a he kaila Ni'ihau paha ia a i 'ole he kaila Kaua'i paha. Ua lohe na'e au, pēlā ka ulana 'ana a kekahi mau kānaka ma Kaua'i. Eia na'e, 'a'ole au i 'ike i kēia 'ano kaila pāpale mai kekahi kupuna mai o Kaua'i. He mea kāka'ikahi ka loa'a 'ana o ka po'e ulana lau hala me ia 'ano pāpale me ho'okahi piko. Ma muli na'e o ko'u 'i'ini e ho'omau i kēia 'imi 'ana i ka 'oko'a o nā 'ano kaila like 'ole no ka ulana 'ana, ua hele akula au i ka po'e i pa'a ka 'ike kupuna no ke a'o 'ana mai ia'u i kēia hana he ulana lau hala. Ua like akula au me ka mana'o o ka 'ōlelo no'eau. " 'A'ohe wāwae o ka i'a. 'O 'oe ka mea me ka wāwae, e ki'i mai." Aia nō ka loa'a mai o ia 'ike a hele aku 'oe e ki'i. Inā 'a'ole 'oe e ki'i i ka 'ike, 'a'ole nō e loa'a mai ana iā 'oe kāu mea i makemake ai.

Ka Hulu Kupuna

E ke hoa heluhelu o nei mo'olelo, he mo'olelo laha'ole kēia e ho'olaha 'ia nei no kēia wahi hulu Kupuna i pa'a ka 'ike o kona mau mākua hānai. 'O Elizabeth Maluihi Lee nō ho'i ia hulu Kupuna a'u e kaena nei i loko o kēia mo'olelo. No laila, ua mana'o 'ia e lilo ia papahana ninaninau e nīnau ai iā ia ma o ka 'ōlelo makuahine, ka 'ōlelo i pū'ā 'ia iā ia mai kona wā pēpē mai a hiki loa i kēia wā. 'A'ohe wā a'u i kama'ilio ai me ia a lohe 'ia paha ka 'ōlelo haole mai kona waha mai, 'o ka 'ōlelo makuahine wale nō kana i kama'ilio ai me a'u. 'O kekahi, 'a'ole au i lohe iā ia i ka 'ōlelo haole. 'O kekahi mea ho'i nāna i 'ume i ka pīhoihoi i loko o'u e lilo 'o Kupuna Maluihi Lee 'o ia ka loea e ninaninau ai no kēia pepa a'u e kākau nei, no ko'u lohe mau 'ana i nā mo'olelo āna i ha'i ai e pili ana i ka ulana lau hala. 'O ka mea hoihoi loa ho'i ia'u i loko o ka ninaninau 'ana iā Kupuna Maluihi Lee, 'o ia ho'i ke kumu no kona ho'omau 'ana i kēia 'ike ulana lau hala. 'Oiai, wahi āna, ua koi wale 'ia 'o ia e komo i loko o ka hana ulana lau hala e kona mau mākua hānai i kona wā kamali'i e a'o mai i ka ulana lau hala no ka pono o ka noho 'ana, eia na'e, 'a'ole 'o ia i ho'opoina a ha'alele i kēlā 'ike. Ua ho'omau 'o ia i ka ulana lau hala i loko o kona ola holo'oko'a no ka mea, 'o ia ka mea e loa'a mai ai ka i'a 'o ia ho'i ke kālā e ola pono ai ka 'ohana. 'O kekahi mea i ola mau ai kēia 'ike ulana lau hala iā Kupuna Maluihi Lee, ma kona kālewa 'ana i ka pāpale ma ka halekū'ai a loa'a mai ke kālā. 'O kekahi mea, ua kuapo lākou i ka pāpale ma kahi o ka mea'ai. Inā 'a'ole i lawa ka 'ai o ka hale, ua ulana 'o ia i ka pāpale a lawe aku i ka halekū'ai e kuapo ai me ka mea'ai. Ma kekahi 'ano, 'o ia kekahi mea e loa'a mai ai ke kenikeni e kū'ai ai i nā pono lako o ka hale a me nā lako o ke kino. Pēlā nō ho'i kā mākou hana kekahi ma Ni'ihau. Inā pono ka lole a i 'ole kekahi pono lako hale paha, ua kui 'ia ka lei pūpū a ho'olilo 'ia, loa'a mai ke kenikeni e kū'ai ai i nā mea a mākou i makemake ai. He kālā ia e ho'olako ai i ka nele o ka 'ohana ma waho a'e o nā kālā i loa'a mai i ko'u makuakāne mai kāna hana 'āina mai.

Ke A'o Kupuna

'O kekahi mea i 'oko'a ai ke a'o kupuna, ma ka noho pū 'ana me lākou a komo pū i loko o ka hana me lākou. Pēlā nō ho'i ko'u a'o 'ana mai i ka hana no ka lei pūpū Ni'ihau. Noho nō ho'i a nānā i ka hana a ko'u makuahine a ho'opili. Ho'omaka 'ia mai ka 'ohi 'ana i ka pūpū. He hana nui ka 'imi 'ana i nā pūpū i ka wā kamali'i. 'A'ole nō i maopopo ka nānā 'ana o ka maka keiki me ka maka makua. 'O ka maka keiki, 'akahi nō a a'o mai i ka nānā 'ana i ka pūpū. Ua komo pū au i loko o kēia hana kekahi. 'A'ole nō i ma'a ko'u mau maka i ka nānā 'ana i nā pūpū a 'a'ole nō i ma'a ko'u lima i ka 'ohi 'ana i nā pūpū. Eia na'e, ma ka hana mau 'ana i ia hana, ua hiki ia'u ke 'ike i nā pūpū a wikiwiki akula ko'u mau manamanalima i ka 'ohi i nā pūpū. Ua like nō me Kupuna Maluihi Lee kekahi. I ko'u nānā 'ana iā ia i ka ulana lau hala, ua 'eleu maoli nō kona lima i ke ki'i i ka lau a ulana. He nui ka hana ma mua no ka lei pūpū. 'O ka wae 'ana, ka 'oki 'ana i ka 'ōkole o ka pūpū, ka 'ōhiki 'ana a puka, ke pale 'ana i ke one. He mau māhele nō e ho'omākaukau mua ai ma mua o ke kui 'ana i ka lei pūpū Ni'ihau. Pēlā nō paha me ko Kupuna Maluihi Lee a'o 'ana mai i ka ulana lau hala. Mea mai 'o Kupuna Maluihi Lee, inā pono nā lau hala no ka ulana 'ana i ka pāpale a i 'ole ka moena paha, nāna nō i hele a pi'i i luna o ke kumu lau hala a ho'oluliluli i ke kumu hala a helele'i nā lau i lalo. Ma hope o ia hana, 'ohi'ohi 'o ia i nā lau āna i lū ai a pōka'a i mau 'ope lau hala a halihali i ka hale. Ma ka hale nō 'o ia i ho'oma'ema'e ai i nā lau hala me kona makuahine hānai. No'u iho, he mea kēia e ho'omana'o mau ana ia'u i ia a'o a ke kupuna ia'u i loko o ko'u ola 'ana. He a'o kēlā i a'o 'ia ia'u e kekahi kupuna loea ulana lau hala a pono au e ho'omau i ia a'o i loko o ko'u kekahi.

'O kekahi ha'awina ho'i a'u i a'o koke ai maiā Kupuna Maluihi Lee mai, nā hua'ōlelo like 'ole āna i ho'opuka ai i kona waha i kona wā i hō'ike ai iā mākou i ka hana lau hala. 'O ia ho'i 'o kīhae, kūka'a, ho'opālahalaha, piko, 'ānoninoni, kū, moe, maka piko, a he nui hou aku nā hua'ōlelo a'u i lohe ai maiā ia mai. 'Oiai, 'o kekahi o kēia mau hua'ōlelo, ma o ko'u kama'ilio wale 'ana nō me ia a 'a'ole nō i ma'a i ko'u lohe pepeiao i kekahi o nā hua'ōlelo āna i ho'opuka mai ai no ka mea, 'a'ole nō ko'u kupunakāne i ho'opuka i kēlā mau hua'ōlelo i mua o'u i kona wā e ulana ana i ka lau hala. 'O kekahi, 'o nā kūpuna Ni'ihau, he po'e ulana makaloa lākou. 'O ka makaloa, he mea kanu ia i ulu i loko o ka wai hapa kai. Wahi a ko'u kupunakāne, i ka wā kahiko, nui nā makaloa i ulu wale ma Ni'ihau. Ua ho'ohana ka po'e Ni'ihau i kona lau a ulana 'ia i moena e hiamoe ai no ka hale. 'Ano makali'i kona lau a 'a'ole pono ka ho'oma'ema'e 'ana iā ia e like me ka hana o ka lau hala. Ua 'ohi wale 'ia ka makaloa a kaula'i 'ia a malo'o a ulana 'ia i moena. 'Oiai, makali'i loa ka lau o ka makaloa, 'a'ole pono ke kīhae 'ana a pōka'aka'a i kūka'a. 'O ka 'ohi'ohi a ho'omalo'o, 'o ia wale nō ka hana e hana ai i ka makaloa. A 'o ia paha ke kumu i ma'a 'ole ai ko'u pepeiao i kēia mau hua'ōlelo kāka'ikahi i lohe 'ia mai ka waha mai o ka po'e ulana lau hala. I ka wā a ko'u Kupunakāne e ulana ana i ka pāpale lau hala, 'a'ole nō au i nīele aku iā ia e pili ana i ka lau hala no ka mea, 'a'ole nō i ulu mai ka hoihoi i loko o'u e a'o mai i ka hana lau hala. I kēia manawa, minamina ho'i ke komo 'ole 'ana mai o ka hoihoi ulana lau hala i loko o'u a e a'o mai i ka hana ulana lau hala ma lalo o ka malu o ko'u kupunakāne i kona wā e ola ana. Aia a hala akula 'o ia i ke ala ho'i 'ole mai a komo maila ka hoihoi i loko o'u no ia mea he ulana lau hala. A pono au e a'o mai i ka 'ike ulana lau hala maiā ha'i mai. 'Oiai, 'a'ole na ko'u kupunakāne i a'o ia'u i ka ulana 'ana i ka lau hala, he mahalo palena 'ole ko'u i nā 'ike i loa'a mai ia'u mai nā kānaka ulana lau hala e ho'omau nei i kēia 'ike. Ma ko lākou ho'omau 'ana i kēia 'ike ulana lau hala, pēlā i ola ai kēia 'ike i loko o nā hanauna e holo nei i kēia au a i ke au e hiki mai ana. 'O kekahi, ʻo nā huaʻōlelo wale nō i maopopo iaʻu i koʻu wā e noho pouli ana, ʻo ia hoʻi, ka lau hala, ke kumu hala, a me ke aʻa hala no ka mea, ua lohe nui ʻia kēia mau huaʻōlelo mai ka waha mai o koʻu kupunakāne ma muli o ka hoʻohana ʻia ʻana o ke aʻa hala i lāʻau lapaʻau. Inā nō paha i hoʻohana ʻole ʻia kēia mau māhele o ka hala i lāʻau lapaʻau, ʻaʻole nō paha i paʻa kēia mau huaʻōlelo i ka papa o koʻu naʻau.

ʻO ka mea ʻano ʻē hoʻi i koʻu manaʻo, i koʻu lohe ʻana iā Kupuna Maluihi Lee i ka haʻi mai he mau mākua waiwai kona mau mākua hānai. I koʻu lohe ʻana i kāna ʻōlelo i haʻi ai iaʻu, noʻonoʻo akula au penei, pehea lā! Inā he mau mākua waiwai kona, mai ke kumu hea mai hoʻi kona ulana ʻana i ka pāpale lau hala a kālewa i ka halekūʻai e kūʻai ai a loaʻa mai ke kenikeni a i ʻole no ke kuapo ʻana i meaʻai? ʻAʻole kēlā ka hana a ka poʻe waiwai! I koʻu manaʻo, inā waiwai ʻoe, ʻaʻole pono ka ulana ʻana i ka pāpale i mea e loaʻa mai ai ke kālā. Na ka poʻe waiwai ʻole ia hana e ulana i ka pāpale lau hala a kālewa i ka halekūʻai e kūʻai ai. Maliʻa, ʻo ia paha kekahi kumu i waiwai ai nā mākua hānai ma muli o ka ulana pāpale lau hala. ʻAʻole naʻe ʻo ia i haʻi mai i ke ʻano o ka waiwai o kona mau mākua hānai. ʻAʻole nō hoʻi ia he hana maikaʻi ka nīele wale ʻana nō iā haʻi i ko lākou moʻolelo pili ʻohana ʻoiai, pili nō ia hana i ke ola ʻohana.

Ke Aʻo Hawaiʻi

Ma muli nui hoʻi o kēia hana, ua komo maila ka manaʻo i loko oʻu e nānā pū i ke ʻano o ke aʻo Hawaiʻi. Noʻu iho, ʻo ke aʻo Hawaiʻi aʻo ʻia ke keiki ma o ka noho pū ʻana me nā mākua a i ʻole ke kupuna paha a komo pū iloko o ka hana i ka wā hoʻokahi. Ma kekahi ʻōlelo ʻana, aʻo ʻia ke keiki i ka ʻike i loko o ka noho ʻohana ʻana. Ma muli o ia noho ʻohana ʻana, ʻaʻohe wā e pau ai ke aʻo Hawaiʻi a poʻohina maoli ke keiki. ʻO kekahi nō hoʻi, aʻo ʻia ke keiki ma ke ʻano he alo a he alo. Nānā nō hoʻi ke keiki i ka hana a ka makua a hoʻopili a pēlā hoʻi ka ʻōlelo kaulana a nā kūpuna, "Nānā ka maka, hana ka lima" (Pukui, 1983). Ua pili nō kēia ʻōlelo noʻeau i ke ʻano o ke aʻo Hawaiʻi. Ma ke komo ʻana o ke keiki i loko o ka hana me ka makua a i ʻole ke Kupuna, ua paʻa maila ka ʻike makua a kupuna i ke keiki. Me ia aku, me ia aku ka hana, a paʻa ka ʻike ma ka papa o ka naʻau. ʻO ka mea waiwai hoʻi o kēia ʻano aʻo Hawaiʻi ʻana, aʻo ʻia ke keiki i kēlā me kēia ʻike Hawaiʻi i loko o ka hana pū ʻana, ka noho pū ʻana, ka ʻai pū ʻana, ka pule pū ʻana a me ka hoʻonānea pū ʻana me nā mākua a me nā kūpuna i ka wā hoʻokahi.

Eia kekahi ʻano aʻo ʻana i ke keiki i ka ʻike kupuna. No ka poʻe Niʻihau, inā he hana kā kekahi kupuna, ua komo pū ke keiki i loko o ka hana me ke kupuna me ke kauoha ʻole ʻia e nā kūpuna a i ʻole nā mākua. Inā loaʻa kekahi hana a nā mākua a i ʻole nā kūpuna paha, komo pū nā keiki a pau o ka hale i loko o ka hana. ʻAʻohe keiki noho wale nō a kūnānā ka maka a me he mea lā 'a'ole maopopo i ka hana. Ua maopopo 'ē i nā keiki inā e kūnānā wale nō ka maka me ke kōkua 'ole i nā kūpuna a mākua paha, 'o ka loa'a maila nō ia i ka pu'u nuku a i 'ole ke pa'i. A 'o ia paha ke kumu i komo wale ai nā keiki i loko o ka hana me ka 'ole o ka leo o nā mākua a me nā kūpuna e kauoha ana i ke keiki e hana i kēlā me kēia mea. He wā nō ko nā mea a pau. He wā e a'o ai i ke keiki a pau ke a'o 'ana a na ke keiki e hana wale nō no lākou iho me ke kōkua 'ole o ka makua. 'O kekahi, 'a'ole pono ke kauoha 'ana o ka makua a i 'ole ke kupuna i ke keiki, "E ke keiki, e kōkua mai!" Inā 'ike lākou he hana kā ka makua, ua komo wale lākou i loko o ka hana. I pololei wale ai ka 'ōlelo no'eau a nā kūpuna. "Kōkua aku kōkua mai, pēlā ihola ka nohona Hawai'i" (Pukui, 1983). Pili nō kēia 'ōlelo no'eau i ke a'o 'ana mai i ka 'ike kupuna. Me he mea lā, he hana ho'ounauna kā ka makua i ke keiki e hana i kēlā mea kēia mea, eia na'e, ma muli o ia hana ho'ounauna i pa'a ai ka 'ike kupuna i ke keiki. A he a'o nohona kanaka nō ia. 'O kekahi, ke hele a pa'a ia 'ike i ke keiki, e mau ana ia 'ike me ia a hiki i kona po'ohina 'ana. 'A'ole hiki ke ho'opoina 'ia. He aha ka noho lō'ihi o ke keiki me ka ho'ohana 'ole i ia 'ike a i ka wā nō e 'upu mai ai ia hana, ua maopopo nō iā ia ka mea e hana ai. 'A'ole pono e nīnau 'ia ke Kupuna, "E tūtū, pehea e hana ai i kēia mea?" Ua komo wale ke keiki i loko o ka hana ma muli o ka pa'a 'ana o ka 'ike ma ka papa o ka na'au o ke keiki. Ua pa'a loa ia 'ike iā ia a hiki i ka luahine a 'elemakule 'ana. Ua pili nō kēia mana'o i ka hana a Kupuna Maluihi Lee. Ua pa'a loa iā ia ka 'ike ulana lau hala a kona mau mākua hānai i a'o ai iā ia. Ma waho o ke a'o Hawai'i, loa'a nō ke a'o haole kekahi.[1]

Ka Ho'olohe 'ana i nā Mo'olelo Kupuna

'O kekahi mea ho'i nāna i hō'oni'oni i ka pīhoihoi o ko'u na'au i loko o kēia hana he ho'olohe mo'olelo kupuna, ma muli wale nō o ko'u noho pū 'ana me nā kūpuna o'u i ho'i i ke ao iā Kāloa mā. No ka mea, nui ho'i ko'u hoihoi e ho'olohe i ko lākou mo'olelo. 'A'ohe wā e ana ai ko'u pepeiao i ka ho'olohe 'ana i nā mo'olelo a nā kūpuna i ha'i waha ai. 'O kēlā mau mo'olelo, he mau mo'olelo ho'ohau'oli, he mau mo'olelo ho'omāke'aka, a i 'ole he mau mo'olelo kolohe paha i loko o ko lākou ola. Mali'a ma muli paha o ko'u noho pū 'ana me lākou a ho'olohe i ko lākou mo'olelo a me kā lākou hana a mau nō kēia hoihoi ho'olohe mo'olelo i loko o'u a hiki i kēia lā. I ko'u mana'o, 'oko'a nā mo'olelo o ka wā ma mua mai nā mo'olelo mai o kēia wā. I ka wā ma mua, nui ka hana a ko kākou po'e kūpuna no ka pono o ka noho 'ana. E la'a ho'i ka mahi'ai 'oe, ka lawai'a 'oe, ka ulana lau hala 'oe, ka 'ohi pūpū a me ka hana pūpū 'oe, ka holoi lole 'oe, ka 'aiana lole 'oe, a me ia mea aku ia mea aku. Nui pū ko lākou noho pū 'ana me ka 'ohana a ha'i i ko lākou mau mo'olelo kekahi. Ma ko'u wā kamali'i e noho ana ma Ni'ihau, ua komo pū au i loko o kēlā mau hana he ha'i mo'olelo e like me koʻu mau kūpuna. Ka haʻi ʻana i koʻu moʻolelo no ka ʻohi pūpū a me ka hana pūpū ʻoe, ka holoi lole ʻoe, ka ʻaiana lole ʻoe, ka puhipuhi ʻaiana ʻoe a me ka hukihuki nāhelehele kekahi ma kula kahi i hoʻolilo ʻia i wahi no ka mahiʻai ʻana i māla ʻai. He mau hana nui nō ia na kekahi keiki e ʻauamo ai. Eia naʻe, he ʻike waiwai nō ia i aʻo ʻia iaʻu a lilo akula ia i moʻolelo naʻu e haʻi ai iā haʻi i loko o koʻu ola i kēia wā makua. A he mea hoʻomanaʻo hoʻi ia mau hana iaʻu i koʻu lohe ʻana i ka moʻolelo o nei kupuna. No ia kumu au e kākau nei i ka moʻolelo o nei hulu Kupuna ʻo Elizabeth Maluihi Lee.

Ka Ulana ʻana i ka Pāpale i ka Lā Hoʻokahi

ʻO kekahi mea hoʻi nānā i hoʻokāhāhā i koʻu noʻonoʻo i ka lohe ʻana i ka ʻōlelo a Kupuna Maluihi Lee, kona ulana ʻana i ka pāpale lau hala i loko o ka lā hoʻokahi. Kupaianaha maoli nō ia hana i koʻu manaʻo. Maopopo iaʻu ʻaʻole loa hiki iaʻu ke ulana i kekahi pāpale i loko o ka lā hoʻokahi. I koʻu nānā ʻana i ka ulana ʻana a ka poʻe ulana pāpale lau hala, ua huikau mua nō koʻu maka i ka nānā wale ʻana nō i kā lākou ulana ʻana. Aia nō a paʻa ka ʻike ulana a laila, e maʻalahi ai ka hana. Maliʻa, ke maʻa koʻu lima i ka ulana ʻana, hiki nō. Na ka poʻe loea wale nō ka ulana ʻana i ka pāpale lau hala i loko o ka lā hoʻokahi. A ʻo ia nō ke kumu no kona nānā ʻole ʻana i kahi a kona manamanalima i kiʻi ai i ka lau hala i kona wā e ulana ana i ka pāpale lau hala. Ua hele a maʻa loa kona manamanalima i ia hana a me ka hoʻomaopopo ʻana i kahi e kiʻi ai i ke kū a me ka moe. A ʻo ia kekahi mea nui aʻu i aʻo ai i loko o ka ulana ʻana i ka paleʻai no ka pākaukau. ʻO ke kū a me ka moe, ʻo ia nā lau e hoʻopihapiha ai i ka puka ma kahi e pono ai. Ke ʻole ke kū a me ka moe, hiki ke ʻike ʻia ka pukapuka i loko o ka ulana ʻana i ka lau hala. I koʻu nīele ʻana iā ia i kā lākou hana ma hope o ka ulana ʻana i ka pāpale lau hala, ʻōlelo maila ʻo ia penei, "Lawe kālewa a i ʻole kuapo" (Elizabeth Maluihi Lee, Kūkā Kamaʻilio, Mei 19, 2012). Ua kālewa ʻia nā pāpale lau hala i ka halekūʻai no ke kuapo ʻana i meaʻai. ʻO ke kanakē ʻoe, ke crack seed ʻoe, ka pelena ʻoe, ka waiūpaka ʻoe a me ia mea aku ia mea aku. I ia wā, ʻono nō ke kanakē. ʻAʻole i haʻi mai nā mākua, ʻaʻole maikaʻi ke kanakē no ke ola kino a ʻoi loa aku ko kākou mau niho. Ua ʻai wale ʻia ke kanakē a ʻo ka hopena, he popopo mai hoʻi kau kahi niho. Eia naʻe, i kēia manawa, ʻōlelo ʻia maila, ʻaʻole maikaʻi ke kanakē no ka niho o popopo auaneʻi nā niho. ʻO kekahi, loaʻa ʻoe i ka maʻi kōpaʻa, ke koko piʻi ʻoe a pēlā wale aku. He nui nā ʻōlelo hoʻokapukapu no nā ʻano meaʻai like ʻole. ʻAʻohe mea pono.

ʻO kekahi, ua kālewa ʻia kā lākou pāpale i ka halekūʻai ʻo Kimura. He halekūʻai pono lau hala kēia ma Kona Hawaiʻi. A kūʻai ʻia nā ʻano pono lau hala like ʻole. ʻO ka pāpale ʻoe, ke ʻeke ʻoe, ka moena ʻoe, ke apolima ʻoe, a me ia mea aku ia mea aku. A kūʻai ʻia nō hoʻi nā pāpale lau hala no nā kumu kūʻai emi loa. A inā kuapo ʻia ka pāpale lau hala no ka meaʻai, ʻo ka pelena ʻoe, ka waiūpaka 'oe, ka palaoa 'oe, ke kini pipi 'oe, ke kōpa'a 'oe a me ia mea aku ia mea aku, emi maoli nō ke kumukū'ai a lākou i ho'olilo ai no nā pāpale lau hala. Inā nele ka hale i ka 'ai, 'o ia nō ka mea i kuapo 'ia a loa'a mai ka 'ai.

'O kekahi mea hou aku āna i ha'i mai ai, kona kuapo 'ana i ka pāpale lau hala no ke kanakē Pākē, 'o ia ho'i ke "crack seed." I ko'u lohe 'ana i kāna 'ōlelo no ke kanakē Pākē, pū'iwa ihola au a no'ono'o ihola au i ka'u hana i ko'u wā kamali'i. Ka hele 'ana o'u me ko'u kupunakāne i ka halekū'ai 'o Ayabe. 'O kēlā halekū'ai, 'o ia nō ka halekū'ai a ka po'e Ni'ihau i hō'ai'ē ai i kā lākou mea'ai. Ua hana 'ia ka 'aelike ma waena o ka po'e Ni'ihau a me ka haku o ka halekū'ai no ka 'āpono 'ana i ka hō'ai'ē 'ana o lākou ma ia halekū'ai. Ua hele a kama'āina lākou i ka po'e Ni'ihau. Ke hele au i ia halekū'ai, 'o kēlā ka mea mua loa a'u i ki'i aku ai, ke kanakē Pākē. 'Ono loa au i ke kanakē Pākē "crack seed." He mea ho'omana'o 'ia kēlā wā i ka lohe 'ana i ka 'ōlelo a Kupuna Maluihi Lee i ha'i mai ai. He 10 kenikeni wale nō no ka pū'olo kanakē Pākē. I kēia manawa, pipi'i loa ke kanakē Pākē. He 'elima a 'eono kālā o ke 'eke ho'okahi. He 'eke li'ili'i wale nō. 'O ka mea hoihoi na'e o ia kuapo 'ana i ke kanakē Pākē me ka pāpale lau hala, emi maoli nō ke kumukū'ai o ka pāpale lau hala i kēlā wā. I kēia wā na'e, pipi'i loa ke kumukū'ai no ka pāpale lau hala. Na ka po'e wale nō me ke kālā e kū'ai i kahi pāpale lau hala. E aho nō paha ke a'o 'ana mai i ka hana ulana lau hala i hiki iā 'oe ke ulana i kou pāpale pono'ī me ka ho'olilo 'ole aku i kāu kālā pono'ī. He hana na'auao ke a'o 'ana mai i ka 'ike ulana lau hala. I kēia mau lā, 'a'ole lākou i kuapo hou i kekahi pāpale lau hala me ke kanakē Pākē. 'O kahi kanakē Pākē, 'o ia mau emi nō a he wahi pi'i iki wale nō. Hiki nō ke uku 'ia me kau kālā pono'ī. 'A'ole nō like me ka pipi'i o ka pāpale lau hala. Mali'a, 'a'ole nō paha i kaulana loa ka pāpale lau hala i ia wā a 'o ia nō paha ke kumu i kuapo wale 'ia ai ka pāpale me ke kanakē Pākē. He mea 'ole paha ka ulana 'ana i ka pāpale lau hala i ia wā. Me he mea lā, 'a'ole nō ia he hana nui. Eia na'e, ke nānā aku i ka hana o ka ulana pāpale lau hala i kēia manawa, he hana nui nō ia. Na wai 'ole ho'i ka hana nui. 'A'ole nō ia he hana li'ili'i. A 'o ia paha kekahi kumu i pipi'i ai ke kumukū'ai o ka pāpale lau hala i kēia mau lā. 'O kekahi, ua 'ike maoli 'ia ka waiwai o ka ulana pāpale lau hala ma muli o ka nui o ka hana. Ua like nō ia hana me ka hana lei pūpū. I ka wā ma mua, ua emi nō ka lei pūpū. 'O ka hana a ka po'e Ni'ihau, ke kipa mai kekahi malihini i Ni'ihau, ua hā'awi wale 'ia ka lei pūpū i ka malihini. No ka mea, 'o ka hapanui o ka manawa, noho ka po'e malihini i laila no ho'okahi pule a ho'i i Kaua'i. A 'o ia ke kumu, i kō lākou ha'alele 'ana iā Ni'ihau, nui nā lei pūpū i hā'awi 'ia iā lākou mai kēlā me kēia 'ohana. 'O kekahi, 'a'ole nō i like kona waiwai e like me kēia wā. I kēia mau lā na'e, pipi'i loa ka lei pūpū a 'a'ole makana wale 'ia aku nō i ka malihini. 'O ka lei wale nō i makana 'ia i ka malihini, ka lei pu'u. 'O nā lei pūpū loloa, 'a'ole i makana 'ia ma muli o ka pipi'i o ia mau lei ala. Ma kekahi 'ano, min-amina nō paha lākou i ka makana wale aku nō i kā lākou lei pūpū i ka malihini no nā kālā he nui e loa'a mai iā lākou ke kū'ai maoli 'ia ma waho. Aia ma kaukani kaukani mau kālā no ka lei ho'okahi. 'Oi aku ka pipi'i ma mua o ka pāpale lau hala. Ma ke kuapo 'ana i ka lei pūpū me ka mea'ai, 'a'ole au i 'ike a lohe pepeiao inā ua hana pū ka po'e Ni'ihau e like me ka hana a ka 'ohana o Kupuna Maluihi Lee. 'O ka hō'ai'ē mea'ai wale nō ka'u i maopopo e like me ka mea a'u i hō'ike aku nei ma luna a'e nei. He mea nui kēia a kākou e a'o ai i nā hanauna hou e ne'e nei i ka nui o ka hana a ko kākou po'e kūpuna ma ka ulana lau hala.

Ka Nui o Nā Pāpale Lau Hala

'O kekahi nīnau a'u i nīele aku ai iā Kupuna Maluihi Lee, 'o ia ho'i, ka nui o nā pāpale lau hala āna i ulana ai. Mea mai 'o ia, he mau hāneli pāpale lau hala āna i ulana ai. 'O kekahi o nā pāpale lau hala, ua ho'olilo 'ia i wahi e loa'a mai ai ke kālā ma waho a'e o ke kuapo 'ana i mea'ai a i 'ole i kanakē. Ma kekahi 'ano, 'o ia ihola nō ka pono o ka noho 'ana. Inā pono ke kālā, 'o ia nō ka mea a lākou i hana ai. Ua kālewa 'ia ka pāpale a kū'ai aku i loa'a mai ke kālā. I kēlā wā, li'ili'i wale nō ke kālā i uku 'ia i ka po'e hana. Eia nae, ua pono nō ka noho 'ana o ka po'e o ia wā. Ua like nō ka hana me ka hana a ka po'e Ni'ihau kekahi. Kui ka po'e Ni'ihau i nā lei pūpū a ho'olilo 'ia i wahi e loa'a mai ai ke kālā e ho'olako ai i nā pono no ka noho 'ana ma Ni'ihau. 'O ke kālā i loa'a mai iā lākou mai ka lei pūpū mai, ua kū'ai 'ia i nā 'ano pono hale like 'ole a me ka pono kino kekahi. 'O nā lei pūpū a lākou i makemake ai e mālama no ka 'ohu'ohu 'ana i ko lākou 'ā'ī, ua mālama 'ia nō e lākou. A like pū nō ia hana me Kupuna Maluihi Lee kekahi. 'O nā pāpale āna i makemake ai e mālama, aia nō me ia. 'O ia nō nā pāpale āna i 'ohu'ohu mau ai i kona po'o. Ua 'ike 'ia nō ka pāpale āna i pāpale ai ma ka wikiō i pa'i 'ia ai. He nani wale nō ia pāpale ona. He nui hou aku nō nā pāpale a 'ano 'oko'a nā kaila o nā pāpale a Kupuna Maluihi Lee i ulana ai. 'O ka pāpale 'ula'ula 'oe, ka pāpale lau hala 'ānoninoni 'oe, ka pāpale lau hala ma'amau, a 'o ka mea wale nō i 'oko'a ma waena o kēia mau pāpale, kona kaila. 'Oko'a nō ke kaila o kēlā me kēia pāpale. Ho'okahi ho'i pāpale āna i 'ohu'ohu ai, ua ulana 'ia i ka lau hala 'ula'ula. 'A'ole au i 'ike mua i ia 'ano lau hala 'ula'ula. 'Ano 'ula'ula a hā'ele'ele kona kala. 'Akahi nō au a 'ike i ia 'ano kala no ka pāpale lau hala. I ko'u nīnau 'ana iā ia, na wai lā i ulana i ia pāpale, 'ōlelo maila 'o ia, nāna nō. 'A'ole o kana mai ka nani o ua pāpale ala. I ka nānā wale aku nō, he ho'ohihi ho'i kau.

Ka Ho'oma'ema'e 'ana i ka Lau Hala

'O kekahi ha'awina ho'i āna i a'o ai ia'u a me kekahi o ko'u mau hoa ma ko mākou hele 'ana i ka 'aha no Ka Ulu Lauhala o Kona. Ua a'o maila 'o ia iā mākou ma kona noho pū 'ana me mākou a a'o mai i ka ho'oma'ema'e 'ana i ka lau hala. I kona 'ike 'ana iā mākou e ho'oma'ema'e ana i nā lau hala i makana aloha 'ia e kekahi Kupuna o Kona, hele maila 'o ia iō mākou ala, a 'ōlelo maila, "E aha ana 'oukou? Ke ho'oma'ema'e nei 'oukou i ka lau hala?" a me kona nānā pū i kā mākou hana i ka lau hala. 'Ōlelo akula au iā ia, "'Ae, ke ho'oma'ema'e nei mākou i kēia mau lau hala." Mea maila 'o ia penei, "E hā'awi mai i kekahi lau hala a hō'ike au iā 'oukou i ka ho'oma'ema'e 'ana." I nānā aku ka hana, 'o kahi manamana lima nō ona kāna i kīhae ai iā waho o ka lihi lau hala, kahi ho'i i milo ai ka lau ma muli o ka malo'o. Ho'omaka koke maila 'o ia e hō'ike iā mākou i ke kīhae a pōka'aka'a 'ana i ka lau hala. I aha iho lā, ua pau nā lau hala a pau i ka ho'oma'ema'e 'ia e ia. Mahalo au i kona noho wale 'ana mai me mākou a a'o mai i ka ho'oma'ema'e 'ana i ka lau hala. He ha'awina kēlā e a'o mai ana iā mākou ka po'e 'akahi nō a komo i loko o ia hana he ulana lau hala. A 'o ia nō ka ha'awina nui e a'o ai inā makemake 'oe e ulana lau hala. Pono e a'o mai i ka ho'oma'ema'e 'ana i ka lau hala. 'A'ole 'o ka hele wale aku nō i ka halekū'ai a kū'ai mai i ka pōka'a lau hala i ho'oma'ema'e 'ē 'ia a ulana i ka lau hala. He aha lā ka ha'awina e a'o ai iā 'oe iho? No ka mea, 'o ka mea nui i loko o kēia hana he a'o kupuna, e hahai ana i ke ala a ko kākou po'e kūpuna i hele ai. Inā he ala ia e kukū ai ka manamanalima i ke kukū, pēlā nō ka hana. Pehea kākou e a'o ai i ka hana nui o ia hana? Ua like akula ia hana me ka houhou 'ana i nā pūpū. Ua komo au i loko o ia hana a ua houhou 'ia ka manamanalima e ke kui hou pūpū. Akā, ke pa'a maila ka 'ike houhou pūpū, pau ihola ka houhou hewa 'ana i ka manamanalima no ka mea, ua maopopo pono ihola i ka hou pololei 'ana i ka pūpū. No ka hana mau hana mau, ua like ia hou hewa 'ana i ka manamanalima i mea 'ole. Ke hou hewa 'ia ka manamanalima no kēlā manawa wale nō ka 'eha. Ke hala aku nō he mau lā, ua ola hou maila ka mana-manalima kahi ho'i i hou hewa 'ia e ke kui. No ka hana 'ana i kekahi lei pūpū loloa, he mau lā a mahina ka lō'ihi e hana ai i ka lei pūpū. Aia nō i ke 'ano o ke kaila i makemake 'ia. Wahi a ko'u lohe maiā Kupuna Maluihi Lee mai, 'o ka ulana 'ana i ka pāpale lau hala, ua hiki ke ulana 'ia i loko o ka lā ho'okahi. 'A'ole nō like ka hana me ka lei pūpū. 'O kekahi, 'o ka lei pūpū, 'oi aku ka pipi'i ma mua o ka pāpale lau hala. No ka lei pūpū loloa, he mau kaukani ke kumukū'ai i kū'ai 'ia ai ka lei pūpū. No ka pāpale lau hala, he mau hāneli wale nō. 'A'ole au i 'ike i kekahi pāpale lau hala i kū'ai 'ia no mau kaukani kālā. Pēlā ka like 'ole o ka hana 'ana i ka pāpale lau hala mai ka lei pūpū mai. No ia kumu, ho'omau 'ia ka loina hana pūpū a hiki i kēia manawa. Pēlā ihola ka hana no ka pono a me ko mākou ola 'ana. 'A'ole i 'ōlelo mai nā kūpuna iā mākou, "E pēpē mā, maika'i wale nō ka noho 'ana!" 'A'ole loa! Ua hana a 'ike maka i ka nui a me ka pa'akikī o ka hana no ka pono o ka noho 'ana. I kēia manawa, mao-popo ia'u ke ola o ka noho 'ana me he kua'āina lā. Mahalo nui au i ko Kupuna Maluihi Lee i kona hele wale 'ana mai iō mākou a a'o i ka ho'oma'ema'e 'ana i ka lau hala no ka mea, ua 'ike ihola au i ka 'i'o o ia hana. Nāu e koho i ke ala e hele ai. E hoʻomau i ia hana a i ʻole e huli kua aku. Noʻu iho, ʻo ka mea e paʻa ai ia ʻike, e hoʻomau aku nō. E like me ka mea i aʻo ʻia e ko kākou mau kūpuna. Inā he ala ia e lōʻihi ai ka hana, ma laila kākou e hahai ai. He mea hoʻomanaʻo hoʻi kēia iaʻu i ka hana a kekahi kanaka i aʻo ʻole ʻia i ka ʻike mai nā kūpuna mai. ʻImi akula i kahi ala e maʻalahi ai ka hana. ʻO ka poʻe Niʻihau, hoʻohana lākou i ke kui e like me nā kui i aʻo ʻia mai ka wā kamaliʻi mai a hiki i kēia manawa. Wahi a koʻu lohe, ʻo kekahi poʻe ʻaʻole naʻe he poʻe Niʻihau, ua hoʻohana lākou i ka makawili i mea e maʻalahi ai ka hana. Eia naʻe, ke paʻa ka lei pūpū i houhou ʻia me ka makawili, ʻōwiliwili ka lei pūpū ke nānā aku. ʻO ka lei pūpū i kui ʻia me ke kui, maikaʻi ka moe ʻana. Kēlā ka ʻokoʻa ma waena o ke kui a me ka makawili. E aʻo mau i ka ʻike o nā kūpuna a e ʻoi mau ka pōmaikaʻi. Pēlā nō ke aʻo ʻana a Kupuna Maluihi Lee. Me kona manamanalima nō ʻo ia i kīhae ai i ke kukū Ma mua naʻe o kona haʻalele ʻana iā mākou i ke aumoe lilo o ka pō, mea maila ʻo ia iā mākou, "E hoʻi ana kēia e hoʻomaha no ka lā ʻapōpō. A hui hou aku nō kākou i ka lā ʻapōpō" (Maluihi Lee, Kūkā Kamaʻilio, Mei 19, 2012). Ma hope o kona haʻalele ʻana iā mākou, mea akula au i koʻu mau hoa, "E, ua ʻike akula ʻolua i kāna hana? Eia nō kākou ke hoʻohana nei i ka ʻohe no ke kīhae ʻana a me ka pōkaʻakaʻa ʻana i ka lau hala, a ʻo kahi Kupuna Maluihi Lee ala, ʻo kahi manamana lima nō a me kona poho lima kāna i hoʻohana ai no ke kīhae a pōkaʻa i nā lau hala. Aloha nō hoʻi ka poʻe maopopo ʻole i ka hana o ka lau hala." ʻO ke kani maila nō ia o ko lāua ʻaka i kaʻu ʻōlelo. Mahalo nui au iā Kupuna Maluihi Lee i kona komo wale ʻana i loko o ia hana a aʻo mai iā mākou i ka hana pono e hana ai ma ka hoʻomaʻemaʻe ʻana i ka lau hala. ʻAʻole ʻo ia i nānā maka wale nō iā mākou na mākou nō e hana no mākou iho nō. Ua hele wale maila ʻo ia iō mākou a komo i loko o ke aʻo ʻana i ka hana e hana ai. A ua aʻo maila ʻo ia iā mākou e like me ka mea i aʻo maoli ʻia iā ia e kona mau mākua hānai. ʻO ka mea pūʻiwa hoʻi iaʻu i kona aʻo ʻana iā mākou i ka hoʻomaʻemaʻe ʻana i ka lau hala, kona hoʻohana ʻana i kona mikiʻao a kīhae i ka milo o ka lau hala. Ua ʻike ʻo ia iā mākou i ka hoʻohana i ka lāʻau ʻohe no ke kīhae ʻana i ka lau hala. ʻO kāna ʻōlelo iā mākou, maikaʻi ka ʻohe no ka hoʻomaʻemaʻe ʻana i ke kukū o ka lau hala akā nona iho, hoʻohana nō ʻo ia i kona mikiʻao a me kona mau lima i mea e kīhae ai i ka lihi o ka lau hala a me ka pōkaʻa ʻana i ka lau hala. He nani ia ʻōlelo i koʻu pepeiao no ka mea, ke hoʻomau nei nō ʻo ia i ke aʻo a kona mau mākua hānai. ʻOiai, ua hana ʻia ka lāʻau ʻohe i mea o hoʻomāmā ai i ka hana no ka hoʻomaʻemaʻe lau hala, eia naʻe, ʻaʻole ʻo ia i hoʻohana i kēlā mau mea i ko mākou wā i hoʻō aku ai iā ia i ka lāʻau ʻohe. Ua aʻo maila nō ʻo ia iā mākou i ka mea i aʻo maoli ʻia iā ia. No ia kumu, mahalo nui au iā ia i ka hōʻike ʻana mai i ia hana iā mākou. ʻO kaʻu nīnau hoʻi i nīele aku ai iā ia, no ke aha mai hoʻi ka hoʻohana ʻia ʻana o kēlā mau lāʻau ʻohe? Mai ke kumu hea mai hoʻi i komo mai ai ka lāʻau ʻohe i mea e kīhae ai i ke kukū o ka lau hala? Mea maila 'o ia, i 'ole e kukū ka lima o ka po'e ho'oma'ema'e lau hala. No'u iho, 'o ka mea ia e ma'a ai ka lima i ka hana. Aia nō a kū mau ka manamana lima i ke kukū a pa'a ka 'ike. Inā 'a'ole kukū ka manamanalima, e makemake ana paha ka mea 'ike 'ole i ka hana ulana lau hala e 'imi i kekahi ala hou aku e kukū 'ole ai kona manamana lima. Ma ke kū'ai 'ana i ke kūka'a lau hala i pau 'ē i ka pōka'aka'a 'ia. 'O ka hana wale nō, he koe a ulana. Ma ke kū'ai 'ana i ke koe 'ohe i mea e kukū 'ole ai ka manamanalima kekahi. No'u iho, mahalo nui au i ka hana a ko kākou mau kūpuna no ka mea, 'a'ole lākou i maka'u i ka hana. Inā he hana ia e kukū mau ai ko lākou manamana lima, ua komo wale aku nō lākou i loko o ka hana me ka nānā 'ole i ka hopena. He mana'o Hawai'i nō ia 'ano hana. E pono e mahalo i ka mea loa'a. Mai pi'ikoi wale aku nō i ka mea i luhi 'ole ai 'oe, 'o ka hopena, e kauka'i wale ana nō 'oe i ka luhi o ha'i. He mea waiwai ke a'o 'ana mai i kekahi hana mai ka ho'omaka 'ana a hiki i ka pau 'ana. He mea ia nou e mākaukau ai a he mea ia nou e mahalo ai i ka hana a kou mau lima i hana ai. He hana nui ka 'ohi'ohi 'ana i nā lau a kāwele i nā lepo i pa'a i loko o ka 'ōmilo lau. Ke pau ia hana, 'o ke kīhae aku i ka 'ēlau a pōka'a i ka lau hala a loa'a mai kahi kūka'a. He ho'okahi lā holo'oko'a nō ia i loko o ia hana inā 'o kēlā wale nō ka mea e hana ai. Pēlā nō e pa'a ai ka 'ike kupuna no ka hana lau hala ma ka papa o ka na'au. Inā nānā 'ole 'ia ka hana nui no ka 'ohi 'ana, ka ho'oma'ema'e 'ana, e no'ono'o ana ka po'e i hana 'ole i ia hana nui, he hana ma'alahi wale nō ia. No'u iho, paipai nui au i ke komo 'ana o nā keiki, 'ōpio i loko o ka hana mai ka ho'omaka 'ana a hiki i ka pau 'ana. Pēlā e pa'a ai ka 'ike ma ka papa o ka na'au a 'o ia ihola ke 'ano o ka nohona Hawai'i. E a'o mau i ka 'ike o nā kūpuna a e 'oi mau ana ka na'auao.

Kā Kupuna Elizabeth Maluihi Lee 'Ōlelo A'o

'O kekahi 'ōlelo a'o a Kupuna Maluihi Lee i ha'i ai ia'u a mana'o au he 'ōlelo a'o ia e pōmaika'i ai kākou nā po'e e 'imi nei i ka 'ike kupuna. Pili nō kēia 'ōlelo a'o i kona ho'olālā 'ana i kēia 'aha 'o Ka Ulana Lauhala o Kona. Mea maila 'o ia, ua ho'olālā 'ia kēia 'ano 'aha i wahi nona e a'o ai i kēia 'ike ulana lau hala i ka po'e e hoihoi ana i ka ulana lau hala. Makemake 'o ia e kā'ana like i kēia 'ike me lākou. 'O ka 'ōlelo ho'i nāna i ho'opā i ko'u na'au i kona 'ōlelo 'ana mai ia'u, inā kāhea mai 'o Iesū iā ia e ho'i i ke ala ho'i 'ole mai, he aha kāna hana me ia makana? He kāka'ikahi wale nō ka po'e i makemake e hō'ike i ko lākou 'ike iā ha'i. E like ho'i me ka 'ike i a'o 'ia iā ia mai loko mai o ka 'ohana. Eia na'e, ua makemake nō 'o Kupuna Maluihi Lee e hō'ike mai i kona 'ike i ka lehulehu no ka ulana lau hala. 'A'ole 'o ia i nānā i kona pono wale nō akā ua makemake 'o ia e kā'ana like i kona 'ike ulana lau hala me ka po'e e hoihoi mai ana i kēia 'ike. Penei nō kāna i 'ī mai ai:

Ina hea mai ana ʻo Iesū iaʻu, e hoʻi me ia? ʻAle hiki iaʻu ke lawe kēlā makana. Ma hea wau? ʻO ia kona makemake, māhele i kēia manaʻo no nā poʻe ʻōpio, ka mea e ʻaʻapo mai ana, makemake mai ana e ʻike i ka ulana ʻana. Pehea e ola ai kēia papahana? Kuʻu ʻike ʻana ʻano kākaʻikahi wale nō ka poʻe ulana. Ua ʻōlelo ʻia au, ʻaʻale pono au e aʻo i kēia i ka lāhui ʻē. . . . Ua hāʻawi mai lākou e hoʻonaʻauao ana iā kākou pākahi a pau loa. Pēlā kākou e māhele aku kā kākou mau mea Hawaiʻi me lākou, ʻO wai ana lākou, haole, Kepanī, Pākē. ʻO wai ana ka mea e makemake e ʻike mai e hoʻōla ʻia ana kēia papahana. E ulu ka aʻa, e ulu ka aʻa maʻō a ma ʻaneʻi. Kū nā kumu. Pua ka hala, ʻala ka hala, pala ka hala, ʻala ka hala, kī ka hala, ai i laila ke ola o ke kumu hookahi. (Elizabeth Maluihi Lee, Kūkā Kamaʻilio, Mei 19, 2012)

ʻO kēia mau ʻōlelo a pau a Kupuna Maluihi Lee i haʻi maila, he mau ʻōlelo aʻo nō ia. ʻO kekahi, ʻaʻole ʻo ia i nānā ʻo wai lā ka poʻe e hele mai ana i mua ona no kēia ʻike āna e kāʻana like aku nei. He hoʻokahi wale nō ona manaʻo ʻo ke kāʻana like ʻana i kona ʻike me haʻi. Mahalo au i kona ʻaʻa ʻana e aʻo mai i kona ʻike me nā ʻano lāhui like ʻole. ʻAʻole i nā Hawaiʻi wale nō akā, i ka poʻe e ulu mai ana ka hoihoi no ia mea he ulana lau hala. I kēia mau lā, ua nui hewahewa nā kumu e aʻo nei i ka ulana lau hala ma ʻō a ma ʻaneʻi. Ke ola mau nei nō kēia ʻike ulana lau hala ma ʻō a ma ʻaneʻi o ka pae ʻāina ʻo Hawaiʻi nei. E like me ka ʻōlelo noʻeau i hōʻike ʻia aku nei ma ka poʻo manaʻo o kēia wahi pepa nei, " ʻAʻohe wāwae o ka iʻa. ʻO ʻoe ka mea wāwae, e kiʻi mai" (Pukui, 1983). Pono kākou e hahai i kēia ʻōlelo noʻeau e kau maila ma luna nei. ʻO ia ka mea e loaʻa ai ka ʻike iā ʻoe, e hele aku i mua o ka poʻe me ia ʻike a aʻo mai i ka ʻike. Nui nā poʻe loea ulana lau hala a Kupuna Maluihi Lee i aʻo ai i ka ulana ʻana i ka lau hala a ke aʻo nei nō ia mau kānaka ma ʻō a ma ʻaneʻi o ka pae ʻāina ʻo Hawaiʻi nei a puni. Mai kali a pau lākou i ka hoʻi me Iesū e like me kā Kupuna Maluihi Lee i aʻo maila iaʻu no kona kāʻana like ʻana i ka ʻike a ke Akua i hoʻopōmaikaʻi ai iā ia. ʻAʻole ʻo ia i mālama i ia ʻike me ia wale iho nō. Ke aʻo nei ʻo ia mai ka poʻe Hawaiʻi a hiki i ka poʻe o ka ʻāina ʻē kekahi. ʻOiai, noho lākou i kahi mamao, eia naʻe ua hele maila i mua o nā loea a aʻo mai i ka hana ulana lau hala. Maiā lākou mai, hiki nō ke hoʻomau a hoʻōla ʻia ka ʻike ulana lau hala o nā kūpuna i nā hanauna hou a me nā hanauna e hiki mai ana. E like me kāna ʻōlelo aʻo i hōʻike maila, "Ulu ka hala, pua ka hala, pala ka hala, ʻala ka hala, kī ka hala, ai i laila ke ola o ke kumu hookahi" (Kupuna Maluihi Lee, Kūkā Kamaʻilio, Mei 19, 2012).

NOTE

1. ʻO ke aʻo haole, na ka poʻe mikionali nō i lawe mai i kēlā ʻano aʻo haole i Hawaiʻi nei. A ʻo ia kēia ʻike e aʻo ʻia nei ma ke kula. Ma o kā lākou hoʻokumu ʻana i ke aʻo haole, pēlā i loaʻa ai i Hawaiʻi nei a hiki i kēia lā. Aʻo ʻia ke keiki mai ka puke mai. ʻAʻole ma ka

noho pū ʻana me ka makua a i ʻole ke kupuna a aʻo mai i ka ʻike makua a kupuna. ʻOkoʻa loa ia ʻano aʻo haole mai ke aʻo Hawaiʻi mai.

NĀ ʻIKE I ʻOHIʻOHI ʻIA

Elbert, S. H., and N. Mahoe. (1970). *Nā mele o Hawaiʻi nei*. Honolulu: University of Hawaiʻi Press.

Pukui, M. K. (1983). *ʻŌlelo noʻeau: Hawaiian proverbs and poetical sayings*. Honolulu: Bishop Museum Press.

Ka Ulana Moena Pāwehe

Lia O'Neill M. A. Keawe

For as long as I can remember, I have admired ulana lau hala.[1] So in the fall of 2011, I did not hesitate to accept an invitation to conduct research on this traditional and customary art form. The invitation was part of an initiative within Hawaiʻinuiākea School of Hawaiian Knowledge at the University of Hawaiʻi at Mānoa (UHM) called Engaging Communities in Education.[2] As a land, sea, and space-grant institution, "the University has a unique responsibility to support, sustain, and expand our engagement with all our communities, and has a particular responsibility to Native Hawaiian communities."[3] Conducting research on ulana lau hala reflects this commitment.

Joining me in this research endeavor were my Hawaiʻinuiākea colleagues Dr. Kuʻuipolani Wong and later Dr. Kekeha Solis, both of whom are instructional faculty at Kawaihuelani Center for Hawaiian Language at UHM. As Kanaka Maoli, we know that with each passing generation of kūpuna, the ʻike of Kanaka Maoli national treasures like pāpale are diminishing.[4] Therefore, our research project, Wehe I Ka Pāpale, was aimed at uncovering or unlocking the ʻike of making pāpale to preserve the generative knowledge that will perpetuate this traditional and customary practice of pāpale for current and future generations of Kanaka.

This chapter is my moʻolelo of Wehe I Ka Pāpale.[5] What started simply as a research endeavor to gather information about pāpale lau hala traditions in Hawaiʻi, through oral interviews, turned into a journey of professional and personal exploration, cultural connections, and identity formation. More than just telling a story, here I engage the art of ulana. From the stories trustingly shared through Wehe I Ka Pāpale, I weave a moena decorated with beautiful pāwehe that are the unique details of each storyteller's life as a practitioner of ulana.[6] It is with permission from and with profound appreciation of these storytellers that I now share the moʻolelo of "Ka Ulana Moena Pāwehe."

Establishing Our Research to ʻĀina

For a little over a year starting in the spring of 2012, our research team created an archive of oral histories by conducting interviews with master weavers and practitioners of ulana. Our interviewees, the storytellers, represented weaving traditions from the islands of Kaua'i, O'ahu, Moloka'i, Maui, and Hawai'i. Each interview offered rich insights into weavers' lives, their background, how they were introduced to ulana, and how they learned to make pāpale, as well as anecdotal information related to ulana pāpale. Our interviews also included questions about resources and materials that were used as well as what weaving styles were engaged to create pāpale.

Aloha I Nā Kumu

As our archive of stories grew, I began to take notice of salient themes and insights that arose from our storytellers about teaching and learning ulana. Many weavers spoke of a deep and continuing gratitude for their kumu.[7] This gratitude is something they now reflect upon, as they themselves have become practitioners or kumu in their own right. As they spoke, some remarked about the pedagogy of their kumu and how they found themselves teaching just as they were taught. Some weavers discussed changes they have implemented now when teaching their haumāna.[8]

Hearing stories about the kumu of these weavers was particularly important because the term "kumu" in Hawaiian has various meanings, which include foundation, source, and origin. From a Kanaka Maoli perspective, it is also fitting to begin our story here as these storytellers establish their connection to mo'okū'auhau,[9] which has created an opulent legacy of ulana lau hala in Hawai'i. It is also a fitting place for us to begin weaving a metaphorical mat, because at the center of our moena poepoe is a piko that links us back to mo'okū'auhau.[10] Later in this narrative, I discuss piko and its other meanings. For now, let me continue sharing what we learned from our storytellers.

The Need for Patience

A consistent theme presented in our interviews about teaching and learning ulana was the importance of patience. Weaver after weaver repeatedly spoke of the necessity to engage patience when weaving. This wisdom was not restricted only to kumu and practitioners, but was also known to haumāna. From the vantage point of kumu, having patience is necessary because students grow and develop in many ways and are a diverse audience. For practitioners, patience is needed because ulana requires that you take your time, be focused, and be fully present (in mind, body, and spirit) in the experience. For haumāna, patience is necessary when learning ulana because you need time to develop and hone skill sets in this art form. Having this understanding early on helps haumāna to clearly understand the insights gained through the learning of ulana. As I listened to these explanations, I began making my own connections to the wisdom shared by these storytellers and wondered if the same explanations could be applied to learning in the academy.

The Transference of Mana

An interesting insight shared among these weavers is the need for the weaver to possess good thoughts while weaving. All weavers who were interviewed felt strongly about this. And all agreed that if the weaver did not heed these words, the energy of the weaver would show up in the weaving. The end result of such weaving would lead to a specific instruction by the kumu to hemo the work.[11] The weaver would have to repeat the weave until smooth. If this dynamic continued, the weaver was then instructed to put down the weaving, literally walk away from the work, and take a break until she or he was calm and relaxed. This was a common thread that weavers shared and is an aspect of weaving they carry with themselves and share with their haumāna. As I pondered this insight, I was struck with a deep curiosity. Could weaving really open up a window into the world of the weaver's emotions? The more I thought about this, the more my curiosity grew. I explored the idea that perhaps this explains how the mana of the weaver is transformed into the weaving.[12] However, because I was not a practitioner of ulana, I was not able to understand the depth of this insight.

A'o Aku, A'o Mai

In interviews with weavers, we wanted to know how ulana is taught and learned in the community. One weaver's response stood out to me because it struck me in a very personal way. This weaver asked me to "imagine a hundred years ago, [when] each Hawaiian household had a weaver."[13] For this weaver, teaching and learning of ulana continues in the same manner as it was taught in the time of our kūpuna—at home. His words were particularly profound to me because I have come to know that our "first community" is, in fact, our family. So his words made logical sense to me. Further, his words caused me to think about the weavers in my own family, and as I did a flood of stories came back to me. First I thought about my maternal grandmother, who would often share stories with us about what a wonderful weaver her mother was. Growing up I distinctly remember her saying, "Oh my mother (my great mother), she could weave anything!"[14] Next, I thought about the stories of my paternal great-grandmother and her great weaving abilities. As I thought about these women, I simultaneously thought about the lost opportunities to learn ulana from them because they had already passed on to the next life. In this reflection, I applied the knowledge of time and history;[15] I gained from my educational experiences at UHM,[16] which provided an understanding of why this knowledge was not passed down from their generation to me. Many times after this interview, I found myself pining over their passing, the loss of their ʻike, and the reality that all I had were stories about what great ulana practitioners they were. Little did I know then that not all was lost. Later I would realize that the stories of these women would become an important part of my life that would lead to the transformation, inspiration, and motivation to learn the ʻike of ulana, to one day reintroduce it into my family for future generations.

Ulana as Addiction

An interesting theme garnered from our interviews was the notion that ulana can be an addiction. Several storytellers spoke of this addiction as an enjoyment, as something therapeutic and relaxing. One weaver warned, "It's a good addiction because once you start weaving, there is a good possibility that you will become immersed in it and then consumed by it."[17] Upon hearing this, I was skeptical and thought to myself, really? Of particular note was a storyteller who explained her addiction to ulana by vividly describing an intense sensation in her fingers caused by merely touching the lau.[18] This weaver explained that the feeling "might be a DNA reaction."[19] Further, she explained, "This calming feeling is sustained as the weaving continues." I found this to be unique and intriguing because no other weaver had provided such a response. Long after our interview had concluded, I kept thinking about this sensation. What did it feel like? I was curious. Again, because I was not a practitioner of ulana, I struggled to understand this experience.

Engaging Protocol

Engaging protocol was a theme that sparked interesting dialogue about teaching and learning ulana. Several weavers discussed how they came to know special patterns or weaving techniques. This occurs when students demonstrate to the kumu that they have achieved a certain level of skill or understanding about the art form. Sometimes, the kumu could simply decide that it is time to pass on knowledge. Nevertheless, there is a distinct method for disseminating this knowledge from kumu to haumāna. The weavers we interviewed received knowledge in the same manner. Equally, they did not teach this ʻike unless they asked their kumu permission to do so, or they were granted permission outright from their kumu to teach it. However, today it seems these cultural protocols are not being perpetuated as they once were in the weaving community.

Weavers shared stories and provided examples demonstrating how protocols are being ignored today. One weaver told of an experience when a kumu taught a couple of haumāna special weaving techniques. The haumāna were explicitly instructed by their kumu not to share the techniques learned unless they asked permission first. Not very long after, the kumu learned that these haumāna had not followed protocol, as instructed, and were teaching the weaving techniques to other weavers without permission from the kumu. Another weaver spoke of an experience when an ulana practitioner attended a series of workshops and learned several weaving designs and patterns. Shortly after the workshops ended, word was out in the weaving community that this individual was claiming authoritative rights to these weaving patterns and designs as their own original work. Still another weaver shared about a new attitude among some weavers in the community, who feel they need not follow any protocols of asking permission to teach, because we are living in a modern Hawaiian society.

As I listened to these stories, I grew angry. Instantly I thought to myself, "Who are these individuals? And how can they be so disrespectful to our kūpuna?" After all, ulana is the 'ike of our kūpuna. As I continued reflecting, I contemplated how I would handle such a situation in my own class at UHM. For the haumāna who disrespected the instruction of the kumu, this is hewa.[20] What I have learned about 'ike kūpuna is that you should, whenever possible, seek permission before using 'ike. Perhaps this explains why formal consent needs to be obtained in the UH system before conducting research.[21] Next, I thought about the practitioner who was claiming weaving patterns and designs from other weavers as original work. Again, this is hewa. In the academy this is called plagiarism, and there is zero tolerance for such actions. Therefore, give credit where credit is due. If the 'ike does not belong to you, cite the rightful author. And for the weavers who want to leave behind the protocol of teaching and learning ulana, this is again hewa. I am embarrassed that these individuals have such bold and brazen attitudes. How quickly they forget whose 'ike they are engaging. My overall response to those creating hewa is reflected in the thought that what is started in hewa can never be pono. Learning 'ike kūpuna is always accompanied with kuleana, whether you realize it or not. So shame on those weavers who are causing hewa.

The Kona Conference

Attending the 2012 Ka Ulu Lauhala O Kona conference marked the culmination of building our archive of oral histories. Upon the recommendation of our storytellers, our research team attended this conference. This would be an opportunity to finally meet the people our storytellers spoke of in their interviews with us, and to expand our oral history archive. In preparation to attend this conference and conduct oral interviews, our research team followed protocol by working with conference organizers to gain approval to conduct our interviews. Once we received their approval, our excitement began to grow. Beyond completing the task of our interviews, our research team was also excited because we would participate in ulana workshops offered through the conference. The thought of actually weaving and making something was indeed exciting.

The conference was held at Keauhou Beach Resort. The workshops were held outdoors on the hotel grounds, under a huge white tent containing tables and chairs. Much like table numbers at a hotel banquet, on each table was a card listing the names of conference participants and the workshop that would utilize that particular table. The workshops were organized according to participant experience and skill set. Because Ipo had experience weaving, she was placed in an advanced workshop. For Kekeha and me, this would serve as our first official weaving experience, so we were placed in a beginner's workshop. Over the next four days, we would participate in our groups with a kumu who would offer us an experience of learning in community through these workshops.

On the initial day of the conference, I carefully looked around, trying to locate individuals by their name tags. As I made my way around the tent, looking for my workshop group, I saw a woman whose name tag identified her as Gwen Kamisugi. She was one of the weavers our team was to interview upon our return to Oʻahu. I introduced myself and through our dialogue found out that she was one of the kumu leading an advanced pāpale workshop at the conference. At the time, I was unaware of the impact this meeting would have for our research team and myself.

In my workshop group, we learned how to make small, simple items like coasters and bookmarks. At the end of the second day, the group wanted to learn to make other items like bracelets and a particular Christmas ornament. Because of this request, it was necessary for our kumu to secure additional lau hala. This need was met when another kumu offered to gather more lau for our group. When the lau was delivered the next day, our kumu took advantage of the opportunity to teach us how to clean the leaves. She instructed each member in our group to take a lau and then walked us through the steps of removing the thorns.[22] I will never forget this exercise because to remove the thorns, you need to be extremely careful to avoid being poked. Unfortunately, I was not so careful and ended up with several thorns in the palms of my hands. Ouch! To eliminate any curling of the leaves, we were then instructed how to smooth out the lau using a tool called a hand roller. This stage was followed by yet another set of instructions to create kūkaʻa.[23] Making kūkaʻa requires that a single leaf be rolled into a tight circle. This process continues as more leaves are added to the kūkaʻa. The leaves are left in this manner until the weaver is ready to ulana. The exact number of leaves in a kūkaʻa varies. Some can have twenty leaves and others might have up to one hundred.

On the same day, a member of Ipo's workshop group gifted her with a bundle of Kona lau. The exact amount of lau was not determined, but the bundle filled up an entire thirty-three-gallon trash bag. What a generous and awesome gift! Through our interviews, we learned that Kona lau is highly valued because of its beautiful color and sturdiness. Later that evening Ipo suggested that we go to the lobby, clean the leaves, and roll them into kūkaʻa for easy transport on the airplane back to Oʻahu. Throughout our initial interviews, storytellers spoke about a unique dynamic that occurs in the evening hours of this conference. We were told, "After dinner, conference participants gather in the hotel lobby to continue their weaving."[24] It is here that relationships are established and developed, and learning continues. Wanting to observe and experience this dynamic for ourselves, we took the bundle of lau that had been gifted to Ipo and headed to the lobby.

When we arrived, we witnessed for ourselves what our storytellers had shared with us. There were kumu and haumāna scattered all over the lobby. Some people returned to their workshop groups to work with their kumu. Others formed groups that were mixed with friends and family. Some worked on their weaving and others were talking, playing music, singing, and dancing hula. It seemed as though everyone was enjoying themselves. Aunty Gwen was there too, doing what we went there to do, clean lau.[25] We found a spot to clean our lau on the periphery of the lobby. Upon closer examination of the lau, we noticed these lau were thornless. I was particularly elated about this news because I had just removed the thorns in my palms from the cleaning lesson earlier that day. So all that we needed to do was wipe the leaves to remove surface dirt, smooth them out, and roll them into kūkaʻa.

Not long after we had organized ourselves and had begun wiping the leaves, a master weaver and mānaleo,[26] Aunty Elizabeth Maluihi Lee, came to join us. Aunty Maluihi greeted us in English and we introduced ourselves in Hawaiian. Without any hesitation she struck up a conversation in Hawaiian with us. We explained that we were from the university and would be interviewing her during the conference. She continued speaking with us and helped us smooth out our lau. At one point she looked at me and watched how I was smoothing out the lau with the hand roller. Then she said in English, "We never had those kine tools. We just used our hand to smooth out the lau."[27] She then demonstrated how this was done by wrapping the lau around the palm of her hand. She continued doing this so we could observe her. She stayed with us for a bit longer, then thanked us for coming to the conference and for wanting to learn ulana. Then she left to return to her room for the night.

The next morning, the three of us returned to our workshop groups for another full day of weaving. While on a break, I ran into Aunty Gwen, who asked how I was doing. She asked if I had woven before. I explained I had not and was in the beginners group. I further explained that our research team was eager to learn but when we inquired with one weaving group on Oʻahu, we were told we would be placed on a two-year waiting list. Aunty Gwen immediately said, "You folks want to learn, when you return to Oʻahu call me up. I'll teach you folks." I couldn't believe what I had just heard. I asked her to confirm what she had just said. Aunty confirmed her response. I thanked her for this special invitation and immediately returned to share this great news with Ipo and Kekeha.

As soon as we returned home to Oʻahu, I called Aunty Gwen, who extended an invitation for us to join her next weaving class. I attended that class and have been weaving with Aunty Gwen and her hui, Na Lālā O Ka Pūhala, ever since.[28] I remain grateful to her for creating an opportunity that has transformed my knowledge base of ulana from that of researcher to practitioner.

Transformation and Reflection

Since weaving with Aunty Gwen and her hui, there have been numerous occasions for me to reflect on the wisdom that was shared through learning in community. Sometimes this wisdom pertains only to the art of ulana. At other times the wisdom is about general life lessons, and then there are times when it applies to both. An example of this wisdom arrived while I was weaving a pāpale. When we weave with the hui, we often situate ourselves in a circle. Aunty usually walks around the group, checking on the weavers and the weaving. One day as she walked around the group she remarked, "Remember, wet your work. You want to make sure your lau stays soft and doesn't dry out and crack."[29] This was a gentle reminder to weavers to take our spray bottles (filled with water) and moisten our lau. I left that day and continued to think about Aunty's words. When I returned to the hui the next time, I shared with her that I had pondered her statement about wetting our work. Aunty quickly said, "It's true. Wetting your work is important." She explained, "In this way the lau hala is so forgiving."

As I did before, I left the hui that day thinking about what Aunty said about the lau. However, as a practitioner now, I think about the process of gathering lau from a completely different perspective. Often the leaves of trees are considered dead when they shrivel up and die. Yet this is the optimal state for the lau in order to ulana. Sprinkling the lau with water certainly brings it back to life, making it supple and flexible once again. I am still fascinated by this process.

I often reflect on this process and think about its application as a philosophy of life. In my opinion, this is an example of art mimicking life.

My transformation from researcher to practitioner of ulana has given me a plethora of opportunities to deepen and broaden my sense of clarity and understanding as I revisit the stories and knowledge shared through the interviews of Wehe I Ka Pāpale. For example, I now understand the need for patience. Beyond learning the project I weave, I am simultaneously learning other elements involved in ulana, like paying close attention to how I hold the strands of lau in my hands. I also need to be mindful of the tension I employ in my weaving. Collectively these things matter because they affect the outcome of your project. All of this requires patience toward building skill and knowledge. I would like to believe that with each weaving project I engage, my tolerance, patience, and knowledge of ulana grows and develops. Equally, as a practitioner I now understand why weavers must think good thoughts and not be stressed or filled with tension while weaving. I have not always incorporated this understanding into my weaving and have seen my naʻau look back at me through my weaving.[30] Also, I have had my own share of experiences when my kumu has said, "hemo," and I have had to undo major portions of my weaving. And after repeated attempts to calm my emotions, I have even had to put down my weaving and walk away until I was calm. And finally I now understand "ulana as addiction." The feeling is awesome! It's a feeling of utter calmness that counters any stress, tension, or anxiety. Through my lived experiences as a practitioner, I better understand the many insights shared by the storytellers of Wehe I Ka Pāpale and can articulate their meanings.

Returning to the Piko

As mentioned earlier, at the center of our moena poepoe is a piko. From a Kanaka Maoli perspective, it is important to understand the purpose, function, and meaning of the piko and its metaphorical significance to moʻokūʻauhau. In her detailed instructions to me about making piko, Aunty Gwen says, "Don't rush. Slow down; take your time and make sure you tie each set of lau firmly so your piko will be strong and not collapse."[31] The wisdom of Aunty's instructions about making the piko strong is significant to me because, "for Kanaka Maoli, the piko is extremely important. We have at least three 'piko.' There is one located on our head, at the fontanel. The second is located at our navel, the third, our genitals."[32] The locations of these piko are also significant because they connect us to genealogy and time. The piko at our fontanel connects us to our ancestors who have journeyed on to the next life. The piko at our navel connects us to our ancestors who are living in current time. And the piko at our genitals connects us to future descendants who have yet to be born. These understandings are similar in ulana as the piko sits in the center of our moena poepoe. It is from this location at the piko that the strands of lau connect with other lau and are bound together through ulana that expands and extends outward the layers of our round mat. As I reflect on this process, I cannot help but see how the art of ulana is mimicking life itself. Nani Wale Ka 'Ikena![33]

Coming Full Circle

I have learned much since the creation of Wehe I Ka Pāpale in 2011. The title of this moʻolelo reflects the depth and breadth of experiences I have gained while conducting this work. The totality of experiences from Wehe I Ka Pāpale have been woven into a beautiful moena poepoe delicately adorned with diverse pāwehe. As I conclude this moʻolelo, I now look at my own experiences as a researcher and practitioner of ulana as part of the pāwehe that adorns this moena. The shape of the moena is intentional because it best represents what I imagine community to look like. Beyond my own findings about teaching and learning in the community, this shape also represents my own journey of professional and personal exploration, cultural connections, and identity formation. I believe I have come full circle in this transformative learning experience. At the start of Wehe I Ka Pāpale, I was the researcher who conducted interviews, collected data, and archived information. Now as a practitioner, I reflect on the information gathered and am able to better understand its purpose, function, and meanings. And as a teacher, this experience has been an opportunity for me to critically reflect on my own practices of teaching and learning in the academy.

Concluding the Journey

It has been nearly five months since I have been able to ulana. The kuleana and demands of negotiating daily life have not provided time for this engagement. However, I now know that I must make time to engage in this activity. I am grateful for this understanding because this is how I spend time with my ancestors through ulana. As I think about my return to ulana, the voice of my kumu comes to me. I can hear her saying,

Look for your three standing kū
Now count from right to left
Bring one strand down and then lock it
Build your next maka and continue on . . .

Don't forget now . . . talk to yourself
Two up, two down, two up, two down
Add your moe, then your kū and continue . . .[34]

Nani wale ka 'ikena
Ka ulana moena pāwehe

NOTES

1. Mary Kawena Pukui and Samuel H. Elbert, *Hawaiian Dictionary: Hawaiian-English, English-Hawaiian*, rev. and enlarged ed. (Honolulu: University of Hawaiʻi Press, 1986), ulana, to plait, weave, 367; lau hala, leaves, 194. Here the reference is to the leaves of the hala tree (*Pandanus tectorius* or screwpine).

2. Konia Freitas, *Hawaiʻinuiākea Community Engagement Institute: Framework and Structure* (Honolulu: Hawaiʻinuiākea School of Hawaiian Knowlege, 2011).

3. Ibid.

4. In this narrative, I use the term "Kanaka Maoli" to mean Native Hawaiians, individuals whose kūpuna were the first peoples of the Hawaiian Archipelago. Pukui and Elbert, *Hawaiian Dictionary*, kūpuna, ancestor, 186; ʻike, knowledge, 96; pāpale, hat, 318.

5. Ibid., moʻolelo, story, 264.

6. Ibid., moena, mat, 250; pāwehe, generic name for colored geometric motifs or designs, 322.

7. Ibid., kumu, teacher, foundation, source, origin, 182.

8. Ibid., haumāna, student, pupil, apprentice, 61.

9. Ibid., moʻokūʻauhau, genealogy, 264.

10. Ibid., moena poepoe, round shape, here referring to a round mat, 334; piko, design in plaiting the hat called pāpale ʻie, 322. This design is also located at the center of our metaphorical mat. Other definitions of piko are discussed below.

11. Ibid., hemo, unfasten, to take apart, 66.

12. Ibid., mana, power, 235.

13. R. Pōhaku Kahoʻohanohano, Wehe I Ka Pāpale interview, Kaunoa Senior Center, Maui, Hawaiʻi, February 10, 2012.

14. Harriet V. Nāpuʻunoa, personal communications, 1980–present.

15. This knowledge includes political histories that explain the assimilation of Kanaka Maoli to Western culture and the effect this would have on future generations. For a discussion, see Jonathan Osorio, "On Being Hawaiian," *Hūlili: Multidisciplinary Research on Hawaiian Well-Being* 3, no. 1 (2006): 19–26.

16. I am deeply grateful for the collective repository of Kanaka Maoli scholarship that has contributed to my understandings of our history, language, culture, identity, and so on.

17. Wehe I Ka Pāpale field notes, January 2012–June 2013.

18. Marcia Omura, Wehe I Ka Pāpale interview, Honolulu, January 28, 2012, and June 25, 2013.

19. Ibid.

20. Pukui and Elbert, *Hawaiian Dictionary*, hewa, wrong, incorrect, 67.

21. Formal consent or approval comes from an authority such as an institutional review board, which protects the rights and welfare of people involved in research.

See "About the UH Human Studies Program and the UH IRB," University of Hawai'i Human Studies Program, accessed October 25, 2013, http://www.hawaii.edu/irb/html /about.php.

22. There are two kinds of lau hala, lau with thorns and lau without thorns. Wehe I Ka Pāpale field notes, January 2012–June 2013.

23. Pukui and Elbert, *Hawaiian Dictionary*, kūka'a, rolled pack, as of pandanus leaves ready to plait, 175.

24. Wehe I Ka Pāpale field notes, January 2012–June 2013.

25. "In Hawai'i, Aunty (or Uncle, for a man) is often used to address a woman from a senior generational line or a generational line equal to the speaker's parents. It is used to show great respect." Marit Dewhurst, Lia O'Neill Moanike'ala Ah-Lan Keawe, Cherie N. K. Okada-Carlson, Marsha MacDowell, and Annette Ku'uipolani Wong, "Ka Ulana 'Ana I Ka Piko (In Weaving You Begin at the Center): Perspectives from a Culturally Specific Approach to Art Education," *Harvard Educational Review* 83, no. 1 (2013): 136–144.

26. Pukui and Elbert, *Hawaiian Dictionary*, mānaleo, native speaker, 236.

27. Wehe I Ka Pāpale field notes, January 2012–June 2013.

28. Pukui and Elbert, *Hawaiian Dictionary*, hui, club, group, 86.

29. Gwen Kamisugi, personal communication, September 4, 2012.

30. Pukui and Elbert, *Hawaiian Dictionary*, na'au, gut, heart, 257. Here I use this term to mean emotions.

31. Gwen Kamisugi, personal communication, September 4, 2012.

32. Dewhurst et al., "Ka Ulana 'Ana I Ka Piko," 136.

33. Beautiful is the view.

34. Gwen Kamisugi, personal communication, September 4, 2012–present.

BIBLIOGRAPHY

Dewhurst, Marit, Lia O'Neill Moanike'ala Ah-Lan Keawe, Marsha MacDowell, Cherie N. K. Okada-Carlson, and Annette Ku'uipolani Wong. "Ka ulana 'ana i ka piko (In Weaving You Begin at the Center): Perspectives from a Culturally Specific Approach to Art Education." *Harvard Educational Review* 83, no. 1 (2013): 136–144.

Freitas, Konia. *Hawai'inuiākea Community Engagement Institute: Framework and Structure.* Honolulu: Hawai'inuiākea School of Hawaiian Knowledge, 2011.

Osorio, Jonathan. "On Being Hawaiian." *Hūlili: Multidisciplinary Research on Hawaiian Well-Being* 3, no. 1 (2006): 19–26.

Pukui, Mary Kawena, and Samuel H. Elbert. *Hawaiian Dictionary: Hawaiian-English, English-Hawaiian*, rev. and enlarged ed. Honolulu: University of Hawai'i Press, 1986.

The Past and Future of Hala (*Pandanus tectorius*) in Hawai'i

Timothy Gallaher

Hala or pūhala is among the most important plants in the ecology and history of Hawai'i and the broader Pacific. Once a major native component of the coastal and lowland areas of Hawai'i, hala forests have been nearly eliminated by human activity, and with them valuable ecological services may have been lost. Hala has also had a profound effect on the people of Oceania. Their use of lau hala sails enabled them to move beyond the reef and become an ocean-voyaging people capable of exploring the vastness of the Pacific. In addition, every part of this tree has uses that have been critical to the cultural heritage and survival of the peoples of this region. Because Hawaiian cultural heritage has been so intertwined with this natural resource, it is important to understand the ecological history of hala, the challenges that have impacted its survival, and the strategies being used to sustain it.

A Botanical Introduction to Hala

In Hawai'i, hala or pūhala refers to species of small, often coastal, trees in the genus *Pandanus*. This includes *Pandanus tectorius,* which is native to Hawai'i, and several more recent introductions. Hala trees are easily recognized by their long, strap-like, and often prickly leaves (lau hala), their aerial prop roots ('ule hala), and their large softball- to basketball-shaped infructescence ('āhui hala), which breaks apart when mature into numerous yellow to red wedge-shaped fruits (figure 8.1). The spiral appearance of leaves along the stem of juvenile trees is a distinctive characteristic, from which the first part of the common name, screwpine, is derived. The second part of this common name apparently refers to the similarities between the fruit of *Pandanus* and that of the pineapple.

The genus *Pandanus* is a member of the plant family called the Pandanaceae. Fossil evidence and molecular clocking using DNA indicate that the Pandanaceae evolved more than 75 million years ago, probably in Laurasia, which consists of present-day Europe and North America (Kvacek & Herman, 2004). At that time, the global climate was much warmer than it is today and Laurasia was a center of tropical plant diversity. The family has since moved southward to the present-day tropics and has diversified into five genera with

Figure 8.1. Parts of the pūhala (*P. tectorius*). A small grove of planted trees (top); infructescence and male inflorescence (middle); a single hala fruit split lengthwise showing the upper flotation tissue, central hard tissue enclosing several seeds, and the lower sweet tissue (bottom left); and the distinctive prop roots of this species (bottom right). Images courtesy of author.

approximately 800 species distributed from Africa eastward to Hawai'i. The center of species diversity is located in the western Pacific. The Pandanaceae are not native to the Americas; however, the sister family to the Pandana-ceae, the Cyclanthaceae, is native to South America. In Ecuador, the leaves of one species of Cyclanthaceae, *Carludovica palmata* (*toquilla* palm), are used to make the Panama hat, which is regarded, along with the Hawaiian pāpale, as the finest plaited hat in the world.

Pandanus is dioecious, which means that there are separate male and female plants. The male trees produce the hīnano, an inflorescence composed of hundreds of small flowers, which releases a copious quantity of pollen (ehu hīnano). Throughout the hīnano are white, strongly scented bracts (modified leaves) that have evolved to attract pollinators; however, the specific animal pollinators are unknown, and experimental studies indicate that, in Hawai'i, the plant's pollen is primarily carried to the flowers of female plants by the wind (Cox, 1985). The female flowers of *Pandanus* resemble a smaller version of the mature fruit cluster. Like the male flowers, the female ones lack many of the more obvious flower parts such as sepals or petals and consist only of the reproductive parts. The various raised black or brown protrusions visible on a *Pandanus* fruit are stigmas, which receive the pollen. The pollen fertilizes the egg, contained within the fruit, which then develops into a seed. Each stigma represents a single flower; however, in *P. tectorius* and other related *Pandanus* species, between three and eight adjacent flowers fuse to form a typical multiseeded fruit or key. Fusing of flowers allows each fruit to contain multiple seeds, which increases the probability that the fruit will include both male and female plants, an important characteristic for founding new populations. Female *Pandanus* trees are also able to form viable seeds even if the flowers have not been pollinated. This process, called apomixis, allows for the proliferation of plants in new areas even when only a female is able to establish. An apomictic female-only population can persist until such time that a male seed or windblown pollen should arrive to reestablish a breeding population (Cox, 1985).

Pandanus is unusual in that its fruit can utilize two separate dispersal mechanisms. The fruit of hala are attractive to animals such as crabs, tortoises, lizards, cassowary, rats, and flying foxes, which have all been observed feeding on the fleshy base of the fruit of various species (Ash, 1987; Bennett, 2000; Cox, 1990; Gaulke, 2010; Lee, 1985; Wiles, Engbring, & Falanruw, 1991). Animals are typically unable to damage the seeds contained within due to the hard bony endocarp (iwi hala) that surrounds and protects the seeds. The fruit of many species of *Pandanus* are also buoyant in water. These species utilize waterways such as rivers or lakes to disperse their fruit, and a few have evolved specific adaptations to the harsh conditions of the sea and coastal areas and rely on ocean drift dispersal. *Pandanus tectorius* is one such species. In addition to tolerating temporary saltwater inundation and the persistent salt spray associated with coastal areas, its fruit are specially adapted to be buoyant on the ocean for long periods of time, and the seeds contained within are unaffected by prolonged saltwater exposure (Guppy, 1906; Nakanishi, 1988). These adaptations have allowed *P. tectorius* to spread throughout the tropical Indo-Pacific to become the most widespread species in the family, with a distribution from eastern Africa to Hawai'i and the South Pacific. Throughout this range, the species has taken on various regional forms, and for this reason several species are sometimes recognized; however, all of them together are known as the *Pandanus tectorius* complex until the precise relationships among them can be more fully understood.

Once a *Pandanus* fruit reaches a place suitable for establishment, the seeds germinate and one to several small seedlings emerge from the fibrous end of the fruit. The stem first assumes a leaning or trailing growth form for up to seven years until prop roots provide sufficient support to allow the sapling to grow upright. This initial growth form may permit several seedlings to survive by allowing them to grow away from one another, thus reducing competition for space (Ash, 1987). After several years, the plant will assume a vertical growth form with limited branching for approximately nine to twelve years, achieving a height of three to five meters (ten–fifteen feet). When grown from seed, *P. tectorius* will begin flowering after ten to twenty-five years, and the production of flowers corresponds with branching. Branching can also be induced; if the growing apex of the tree is diseased or suffers physical damage, dormant buds along the stem can develop new branches, and some of these may develop into plantlets complete with roots (Gallaher, personal observation). *Pandanus tectorius* can grow to a maximum height of nine meters (thirty feet) and may live approximately sixty years (Ash, 1987). Of nine hala trees planted (presumably as several-year-old saplings) at Webster Hall on the University of Hawai'i at Mānoa campus in 1961, four remain today (fifty-two-plus years old), and these have the appearance of very old trees (Krajina, Rock, & St. John, 1962).

The leaves of *Pandanus* contain a wide array of natural plant chemicals, including pigments and phenolic compounds such as tannins (Kumar et al., 2010; Londonkar & Kamble, 2009). These chemicals accumulate in the growing leaves over time and act to deter the activity of insects and fungi. Some of the chemicals contribute to the red or brown color of the dried leaves, while the density of fibers contributes to the durability and pliability of the leaf. Variations in these leaf characters determine the suitability of the leaf for plaiting (Gwen Kamisugi, personal communication, March 2, 2013). A cross-section of a leaf (figure 8.2) reveals an upper and lower leaf epidermis, which produces a waterproof wax, and a regular pattern of fibrous vascular bundles that extend from the upper to lower epidermis, imparting strength to the leaf. Between

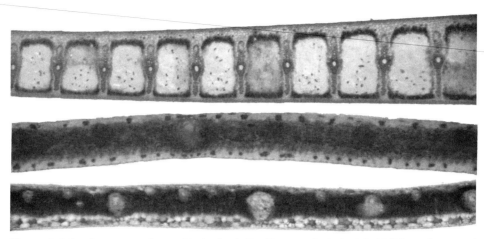

Figure 8.2. Leaf cross-sections of hala (top), the Panama hat plant (middle), and coconut (bottom). Fibers have been stained dark. This comparison illustrates the unique structural features of hala, particularly the regular arrangement of vascular bundles and storage cells. Images courtesy of author.

these bundles are nearly clear larger cells where water and leaf chemicals are stored, surrounded by darker cells where photosynthesis occurs. The clear storage cells are absent from the much thinner leaves of coconut and the *toquilla* palm. Variation in the mechanical and chemical properties of lau hala likely has a genetic basis and, out of this natural variation, lau hala practitioners have selected favored trees with exceptional leaf quality. Some practitioners have also observed that the habitat in which the trees grow (e.g., at the beach versus in the mountains) has a marked effect on the texture and workability of the leaves, indicating an environmental component to the natural variation (Gwen Kamisugi, personal communication, March 2, 2013).

As hala trees age, they produce smaller leaves and infructescences and prop roots grow out from the terminal leaf clusters. If these branches should break off, perhaps during strong winds, the entire terminal cluster of leaves and roots can form a new plant. This terminal cluster is commonly cut from mature trees and used for vegetative propagation by people throughout the Pacific. This method of propagation ensures that the resulting tree will have properties similar to the parent tree. Hala is also propagated by seed; however, the resulting plant may have a different genetic makeup and therefore different leaf or fruit qualities than the mother plant.

Hala in Prehuman Hawai'i

Pandanus tectorius evolved approximately 2 to 4 million years ago along the coast of Queensland, Australia, out of a group of Australian endemic species that inhabit various inland watercourses such as rivers, ephemeral streams, and swamps (Gallaher et al., unpublished data). From those origins, the species has spread throughout the tropical Indian and Pacific oceans following ocean currents (Gallaher, unpublished data). Ancient (over 1.2 million years old) fossils of *Pandanus* fruit found on the north shore of Kaua'i provide the evidence that this species first floated to the shores of Hawai'i without the aid of humans (Cunningham, 1994). In addition to hala, *Freycinetia arborea,* or 'ie'ie, is an indigenous liana (woody vine) of the Pandanaceae that is pollinated and dispersed by birds and mammals and can be found growing on trees in wet interior forests in Hawai'i and in the South Pacific.

Pandanus tectorius is often among the first plants to colonize the shores of tropical Pacific islands. For example, *P. tectorius* was already well established fourteen years after the 1883 eruption of Krakatoa "sterilized" the nearby island of Rakata, and the species was recorded on Anak Krakatau in 1934, only three years after the initial emergence of that island (Whittaker, Bush, & Richards, 1989).

In Hawai'i, hala is often an important component of relatively recent lava flows, although 'ōhi'a (*Metrosideros polymorpha*) is typically the first flowering plant to establish itself, due in part to its dustlike seeds, which are rapidly dispersed in the wind. Over time, hala may establish particularly in coastal areas and tends to replace 'ōhi'a, likely due to a higher tolerance of salinity (Atkinson, 1970).[1] Once established, *P. tectorius* can form dense groves with few other species present. This is in part due to the species' ability to inhabit poor rocky soils and areas with moderate slope. In addition, the leaves of *P. tectorius* break down slowly over time, resulting in the buildup of a significant leaf litter layer that may inhibit the germination of competitor species.[2] Over long time scales, and particularly in inland areas where *Pandanus* does not benefit from its competitive advantage of salinity tolerance, *Pandanus* forest will eventually be replaced by more long-lived species. In Hawai'i, this would typically include mixed 'ōhi'a and koa (*Acacia koa*) forests, which represent the more stable long-term dominant vegetation type in Hawai'i. *Pandanus* may continue to be a part of these forest assemblies, particularly along streams and in areas with a moderate degree of slope.

Large, naturally occurring coastal hala forests were once widespread along windward areas of Hawai'i. In some cases, these populations extended many miles inland, reaching elevations up to 610 meters (2,000 feet; Wagner, Herbst, & Sohmer, 1999).[3] Remnants of these hala forests can still be found on O'ahu, Hawai'i Island, Maui, Moloka'i and Kaua'i. On windward O'ahu, the remnants of a once-larger hala forest can be found from 'Olomana and through the valleys and ridges of the Ko'olau mountain to Punalu'u or even farther north at an elevation of 120 to 450 meters (400–1,000 feet). At its southerly most point, the band of scattered hala trees extends to near the base of the Nu'uanu pali, where the hala grove known as Nā Hala o Kekele, which has figured prominently in several chants and legends, was once located. At the high-elevation Ka'au crater on the island of O'ahu, *Pandanus* pollen is found throughout the 28,000-year pollen record. Presumably the pollen was blown up into the Ko'olau mountain range from the windward *Pandanus* forests. *Pandanus* pollen appears only as a trace, however, in the 3,000-year record of the coastal Kawainui marsh, indicating that the windward *Pandanus* forests of O'ahu may not have extended completely to the coasts in the drier areas such as in South Kāne'ohe, Kailua, or Waimānalo but was somewhat confined to coastal or inland areas with higher annual rainfall (Athens & Ward, 1991, 1993; Hotchkiss & Juvik, 1999).

Based on occurrence data of natural populations of *P. tectorius* throughout the Pacific, hala thrives in areas with annual rainfall greater than about 1,200 mm (forty-seven inches) and minimum temperatures above 10°C (50°F; Gallaher, unpublished data; figure 8.3). Hala can survive in drier areas if there is an adequate supply of near-surface groundwater. Certainly other environmental factors limit the natural distribution of hala in Hawai'i, and the actual distribution would be further restricted by limitations of seed dispersal into upland areas and by competition with other native species.

Pandanus and People

The genus *Pandanus* includes many species that are useful to people around the world, and humans have a long history with the plant. In addition to the leaves, which were and continue to be the most widely used natural fiber material in Oceania, nearly every part of the plant has important uses. The role of hala in several aspects of Hawaiian material culture and in expressive oral traditions is explored by other contributors to this volume; however, a few examples from throughout Oceania are also discussed here.

In addition to the ubiquitous use of leaves in plaited items, the large prop roots were a source of fibers that could be separated by beating and fashioned into thread or rope (Summers, 1990). The large above-ground root tips were a source of traditional medicine, and the trunks of large trees are still used as posts for houses and as the main structural supports for much larger structures.[4] Throughout Oceania, the highly fragrant male inflorescence is associated with sexuality and promiscuity, and the scented floral bracts, along with the soft and copious quantity of pollen that is produced, are considered an aphrodisiac.

The fruit of several species of *Pandanus* continues to be an important staple food throughout the Pacific. *Pandanus conoideus* from New Guinea produces a

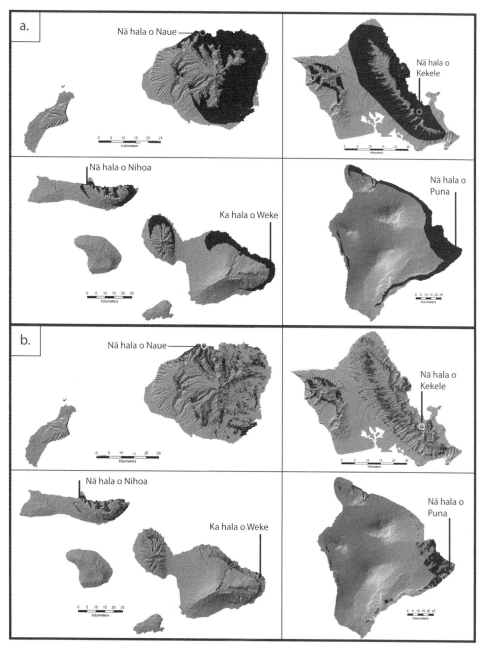

Figure 8.3. Potential distribution of hala in Hawai'i (darkened areas) and some of the named hala groves. The potential distribution is based on the rainfall and temperature tolerances of *P. tectorius* based on data from throughout its natural range. Geospatial climate data from the *Rainfall Atlas of Hawai'i* (Giambelluca et al., 2012) and the Prism Climate Group (Daly and Halbleib, 2006).

fruit, high in beta-carotene, which is eaten raw or processed into an array of food and beverage products. *Pandanus brosimos, P. julianettii,* and *P. dubius* produce edible seeds, and *P. amaryllifolius* has aromatic leaves used in Southeast Asian cuisine (Hyndman, 1984; Teng, Shen, & Goh, 1979; Yen, 1993). Some of the earliest evidence for human habitation in the Pacific comes from 34,000–36,000-year-old sites in the New Guinea highlands. Charred remains from these sites suggest that *Pandanus* was an important food source for the earliest New Guineans in areas where food resources were otherwise limited (Summerhayes et al., 2010).

The fruit of *P. tectorius* played a similar role in the human colonization of the resource-limited atolls of the central Pacific. In Kiribati and the Marshall Islands, *Pandanus* remains a staple food source providing nutrients that are a limiting factor for human populations, given the relatively few plant species that can survive the poor coralline atoll soils. While the fruit of all *P. tectorius* is edible, most wild plants, including those in Hawai'i, have calcium oxalate crystals in their fruit tissue. This is similar to the compound found in kalo (*Colocasia esculenta*). The crystals are irritating or painful if the raw fruit is consumed; however, they can be removed by cooking. In the central Pacific, however, many cultivated varieties of *P. tectorius* have been developed that are larger and less fibrous than wild forms and that have significantly less calcium oxalate, such that they can be eaten raw.[5] These varieties are also much more nutritious than wild forms, with up to ten times the usual amount of beta-carotene, which is an essential yet otherwise rare nutrient in the diets of atoll people (Englberger et al., 2007; Englberger, Aalbersberg, Fitzgerald, Marks, & Chand, 2003). In addition to its central role as a food source, over fifty additional uses of *Pandanus* have been recorded on the atolls of the central Pacific (Thaman, 1992). The importance of *Pandanus* on Pacific atolls is also indicated by the hundreds of named cultivated varieties that can be found on these small islands.

Probably the most important use of *Pandanus*, and one that is often overlooked, is the use of lau hala to make lā or pe'a (canoe sails). While paddling canoes large and small were used for short-distance travel, near-shore fishing, reef gathering, and recreational activities throughout the Pacific, these smaller canoes were rarely used for interisland travel. For long-distance voyages, the people of Oceania relied primarily, if not exclusively, on sailing vessels with sails made from lau hala. Such canoes were ubiquitous throughout both Polynesia and Micronesia. In Hawai'i, the sails were made from plaited lau hala strips that were lashed together and to the mast with rope made from 'olonā (Haddon & Hornell, 1936; *Touchardia latifolia*). Micronesians and Polynesians used these vessels to sail to virtually every island and remote archipelago in the tropical Pacific, possibly reaching South America (Balter, 2010; Jones,

Matisoo-Smith, & Ramirez-Aliaga, 2011). In a few cases, however, these appear to have been one-way voyages. Hala was not able to establish on either Rapa Nui (Easter Island) or in Aotearoa (New Zealand). The lack of lau hala to make new sails may have resulted in the isolation of the communities on these outposts of Polynesia and may have had an important impact on the development of those societies.

Hala in Hawai'i Following Polynesian Arrival

Over a million years after hala established itself on the shores of Hawai'i, the first Hawaiians arrived on voyaging canoes powered by the wind caught in lau hala sails. Those first human voyagers most likely carried hala seeds or branches with them in order to establish groves of the plant and ensure a future supply of the valuable leaves. Hala is therefore considered to be both an indigenous (native) plant in Hawai'i and a "canoe plant" or Polynesian introduction.

In order to accommodate human occupation following the arrival of the first Hawaiians, some of the natural forest had to be removed to make way for habitation and agricultural activities, chiefly taro. For example, in 1789, Captain Portlock described the lowlands and valleys of Kāne'ohe as being in a "great state of cultivation." Clearing by Hawaiians, through either manual methods or the use of fire, may have directly impacted and in some cases isolated widespread hala forests from their coastal origins to valley interiors and to areas protected by cultural proscriptions. By one estimate, up to 10 percent of the total estimated potential area of hala may have been impacted by intensive Hawaiian agricultural activities (Ladefoged et al., 2009).

People in Hawai'i and throughout the Pacific may have promoted *Pandanus* by influencing natural fire regimes or by using fire to clear unwanted vegetation. *Pandanus,* which has a tolerance for fire, would have thrived in these recently cleared areas. An increase in *Pandanus* pollen following human establishment is evident at Avai'o'vuna Swamp in Vava'u, Tonga (Fall, 2005) and Tukou Swamp in Rapa, French Polynesia (Prebble & Dowe, 2008). Similarly, in Mangaia in the Cook Islands the expansion of hala as a dominant vegetation type was likely influenced by burning of other vegetation types (Kirch, 1996). At Rimatara, in the Austral Archipelago (French Polynesia), however, the pollen record indicates a prehuman habitat dominated by *Pandanus,* followed by a sudden increase in both charcoal and taro (*Colocasia*) pollen and a reduction in *Pandanus* pollen, indicating that the area was converted from *Pandanus* forest to taro agriculture. *Pandanus* pollen and macrofossils such as leaves and fruit became more abundant at Māhā'ulepū, Kaua'i, following Polynesian settlement, indicating that the early Hawaiians either directly or indirectly promoted the spread of hala in some cases (Burney et al., 2001).

Whether the total extent of *Pandanus* increased or decreased in Hawai'i following the arrival of Polynesians is unknown; however, the naming of hala groves may be one indication that the value of maintaining groves as a resource was recognized and may also indicate some degree of protection for these natural resources under traditional resource management systems. Named hala groves or place names that include reference to hala can be found on all of the islands of Hawai'i capable of supporting hala forests. Puna on Hawai'i Island was also known as Puna Paia'Ala i ka Hala (Handy, Handy, & Pukui, 1972, p. 200; Puna Hedged with Fragrant *Pandanus*), and early European accounts suggest that hala forests on the eastern coast of that island were widespread and extended many miles inland from Hilo to Kea'au (Wilkes, 1845). In Hāna, Maui, an extensive coastal hala forest was known as Kahalaoweke (Kamakau, 1961, p. 30). Nā Hala o Nihoa referred to a hala grove above Kalaupapa, Moloka'i. Nā Hala o Naue, at Hā'ena, Kaua'i, and Nā Hala o Kekele on O'ahu have figured prominently in several legends and chants.

In Hawai'i, several varieties of hala were recognized and named (see Meilleur, Maigret, & Manshardt, 1997, p. 24). Some of the names may refer to varieties brought by Hawaiians from elsewhere in Polynesia, while others may refer to unique forms that first evolved in Hawai'i and were recognized for some interesting physical characteristic. It is unclear whether specific varieties were propagated and perpetuated along with other useful plants or if the varietal names refer to forms that were observed from natural groves. The Hawaiian names for hala and other useful plants often used a binomial (two-name) system. Examples include hala 'ula (red *Pandanus*) or hala melemele (yellow *Pandanus*), referring to the color of the ripe fruit. This descriptive naming system is consistent with those used by many other traditional cultures around the world and with the system used by botanists and other biologists.

Hala in Hawai'i after European Contact

The arrival of Europeans in Hawai'i and the corresponding shift in value systems and resource requirements had significant effects on all of the natural resources of Hawai'i, including hala. Natural or managed lowland forests were replaced by new agricultural activities. Chief among these were the introduction of cattle and other livestock such as sheep and goats, sugar, coffee, rice, and pineapple (Devaney, Kelly, Lee, & Motteler, 1982). While sugar and rice cultivation dominated the lowlands, coffee and pineapple could be cultivated on terraced hills and the backs of valleys. Cattle, goats, and sheep were sometimes managed on pastures but were often allowed to roam freely through native forests and agricultural lands alike.

The history of the hala grove of Kekele represents an interesting case study in the changing practices of land management in Hawai'i. In 1821, Hiram Bingham referred to a "dense wood" at the base of the Nu'uanu pali in the area known as Nā Hala o Kekele (Bingham, 1849, p. 131). In 1839, the land was leased by King Kamehameha III and Ka'ahumanu III to Boaz Mahune, Jona Pi'ikoi, and others to be used as cattle pasture. Some portion of the hala grove was still present in November 1846, as seen by a crew member of the Danish ship *Galathea*, who descended the pali through a *"Pandanus* thicket" and emerged upon a clearing owned by "Pikuiha" (possibly Jona Pi'ikoi), which was occupied by numerous cattle (Bille, 1852, p. 269). The "Great Māhele" of 1848, which instituted private land ownership, was followed by foreign land ownership in 1850. The lands of Kekele, now divided, changed hands several times and were the subject of an 1857 Hawai'i Supreme Court case, where it was established that cattle had been run over the land (Davis, 1866). A visitor to Hawai'i in 1853 observed that the plains below the Nu'uanu pali had been cleared, stating, "Hundreds of cattle may be seen feeding on the rich pasture with which these plains are covered" (Bates, 1854, p. 104). A similar observation was published in a Hawaiian newspaper in 1866: "Kekele is the land just below Nu'uanu, so fragrant with the *hala* blossoms and fruit used for leis. It was a rich land a while ago but now there are not many plants because animals (cattle, horses, etc.) are permitted there" (Sterling & Summers, 1978). Following the abandonment of agriculture in the 1950s, the area where Nā Hala o Kekele was once located is today covered with secondary forest dominated by alien species and developed areas occupied by golf courses and houses.

The other named hala groves in Hawai'i have faced similar challenges. Nā Hala o Naue at Ha'ena Kaua'i is gone today. Many of the trees were killed by the April 1, 1946, tsunami with subsequent suburban development taking over areas where the forest may have reestablished itself (Shepard, MacDonald, & Cox, 1950). A mixed forest that includes hala, however, can still be found in nearby Hanakapiai valley. A few tracts of hala forest can still be found along the coast in Puna on Hawai'i Island, although sugarcane followed by the encroachment of invasive species and subsequent development has replaced much of the hala forest (Brigham, 1906). Large groves of hala can still be found at Nihoa above Kalaupapa, Moloka'i, and in nearby areas (Bill Garnett, personal communication, 2013).

In many of the coastal areas of Hawai'i where hala was once likely a dominant species, two invasive species now directly compete with *Pandanus* for habitat. The Pacific almond (*Terminalia cattappa*) was first introduced to Hawai'i prior to 1923, and ironwood (*Casuaraina equisetifolia*) was introduced in the 1890s and extensively planted in the twentieth century based on the notion that it would provide protection from shoreline erosion (Kaufman & Gallaher, 2011; Wagner et al., 1999).

At Hāna, Maui, large coastal hala forests can still be found, although they are under imminent threat by the invasive scale insect *Thysanococcus pandani*, which was accidentally introduced to the area, likely on material imported to one of the botanical gardens. Prior to this, the scale was known only from Java and Singapore.

The scale insect covers the leaves and fruit of *Pandanus* and feeds on sugars in the plant, weakening or sometimes killing adult plants (Stickney, 1934; figure 8.4). Young plants are quickly killed and in any case the leaves of hala trees infested with the scale are rendered useless to hala plaiters. Although this scale is a wingless insect, it likely spreads by blowing through the air from plant to plant and may also be dispersed by people who transport infested leaves or fruit. The scale was first observed in Hāna in November 1995, and by October 1996 it occupied a half-mile strip along the coast. The scale reached Ke'anae by November 2002 and was found on the offshore islets of Keopuka, Moku Huki, and Pu'u Kū in 2005 (Starr, Starr, & Wood, 2006). The scale has presently spread to virtually all areas of Maui. On September 25, 2013, the hala scale was identified by lau hala practitioners on cultivated hala plants on O'ahu. At this time, the extent of the scale infestation on O'ahu is unknown.

Between 2003 and 2006, *Pandanus* scale was intercepted on five occasions by agricultural inspectors in Los Angeles County, California. All of these were found on tropical flower shipments originating from Maui (County of Los Angeles, 2004; Gevork Arakelian, senior biologist, Los Angeles County, personal communication, 2013). Due to funding and staff limitations, the state of Hawai'i is not able to provide inspection services for interisland shipments, and there are currently no official restrictions on the import of infected *Pandanus* material from Maui (or O'ahu) to other islands. In addition, there are no known effective measures to combat or control the scale (Darcy Oishi, State Department of Agriculture, personal communication, 2013).

The Hawai'i Department of Agriculture has begun to search for a biocontrol for the hala scale. The first step of this process will be a search within the native range of the scale for a natural enemy such as a parasitic wasp or predator ladybug that exclusively parasitizes or feeds upon *Thysanococcus*. Once a candidate predator or parasites are found, testing will be done in the native range before regulatory approval is sought to conduct subsequent testing and finally controlled release of the biocontrol in Hawai'i. Any candidate biocontrol must be effective in controlling the scale insect and must not negatively impact any native or commercially important organisms in Hawai'i. Funding has been obtained by the State Department of Agriculture to begin to address the hala scale problem, and the timeline for these efforts is four to six years

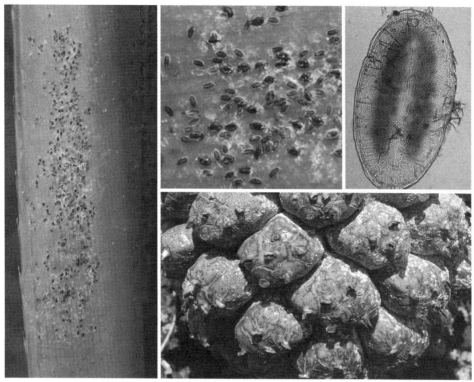

Figure 8.4. The *Pandanus* scale, *Thysanococcus pandani*, on leaves (top) and fruit (bottom) of hala at Hāna, Maui. Left: a close-up of the scale insects. Images courtesy of author.

following the identification of suitable biocontrol candidates (Darcy Oishi, personal communication). If the biocontrol program is unsuccessful, the full impact of the scale will be felt within the next few decades as the mature hala trees from the last remaining hala forests in Hawai'i reach the end of their life span.

By 1900, three additional species of *Pandanus* had been introduced to Hawai'i (Thrum, 1900), and a variegated *Pandanus* was commonplace by 1915 (Bryan, 1915). The introduced *P. baptistii,* believed to be native to New Britain Island in Papua New Guinea, lacks leaf prickles (unarmed) and is variegated or may revert to an all-green form. This all-green form, or perhaps another variety with occasional white variegation along the leaf margins, became a favored variety used by lau hala practitioners known as kilipaki (literally, Kiribati or the Gilbert Islands; Gwen Kamisugi, personal communication, March 2, 2013). The unarmed, all-green *P. baptistii* is today becoming a popular plant, often replacing native armed *P. tectorius* in the urban landscape. These have been planted on the University of Hawai'i at Mānoa campus to replace the older Hawaiian hala. Several other species can be found today in botanical gardens and private residences, including the wide-leafed *P. dubius* from the western Pacific. Some lau hala practitioners actively seek out and experiment with these new introductions to find leaves with desirable color, strength, and texture.

Over the past 200 years, the combined effects of agriculture, land development, deforestation, and the introduction of invasive species have had dramatic consequences for the native species of Hawai'i. These modern factors have reduced the total potential area for hala forest in Hawai'i to approximately 33 percent of the total prehuman potential (figure 8.3.b). An analysis of actual vegetation types in Hawai'i found that the total area of *Pandanus* forest is approximately nine or ten square kilometers, or approximately 1 percent of the total potential habitat (Gon et al., 2006). Further, most of the remaining hala forest is on the island of Maui and is threatened by the invasive scale.

The Future of Hala in Hawai'i

Despite the threats, *P. tectorius* is a very resilient species. Unlike many of the native species in Hawai'i, the survival of the species is not currently threatened. As an important ecological component of the natural environment and as a natural cultural resource, however, hala in Hawai'i is threatened. Changing values, resource needs, and cultural systems have removed any protections on historical named groves and favorite trees. Adequate supplies of lau hala that meet the stringent quality thresholds applied by practitioners are lacking, and leaves for use in plaiting are now being imported from other countries, including Tahiti and the Philippines. Faced with these threats, lau hala practitioners have taken on the role of resource managers. Lau hala groups actively manage trees, and at least one group has begun to establish new groves. The kumu (teachers) of these groups are educating a new generation of practitioners, not only in the painstaking skill of plaiting lau hala but also in the process of propagating and tending hala trees. They are learning how to recognize the natural diversity within the resource and select the trees and leaves that will produce the highest-quality results. As more individuals become aware of the growing threats to sustaining this resource so important to Hawaiian culture, it is hoped that even more solutions will be found to protect, nurture, and restore hala to levels needed to ensure sustainability of the resource and the cultural features it supports. Another positive development is the use of hala trees in coastal and riparian (riverbank) restoration and erosion control programs. *Pandanus* has also been recommended for planting along suitable shorelines for protection from the effects of erosion, storm surge, and tsunami (Nandasena, Tanaka, & Tanimoto, 2008). Hala is easy to grow and once established will perpetuate itself quite readily. Replanting and adequate management along with protection from the scale insect will ensure that hala will thrive in Hawaiʻi both as an important ecological resource and as a treasured cultural resource.

Acknowledgments

Mahalo to Gwen Kamisugi and the lau hala practitioners of Nā Lālā o ka Pūhala for sharing information for this chapter. Special thanks to James Ishimoto for assistance conducting fieldwork and to botanist Jeff Boutain for useful conversations and assistance in imaging lau hala cross-sections. Thegn Ladefoged generously provided GIS layers. I also thank the editors for their invaluable contributions and two anonymous reviewers for their comments and suggestions.

NOTES

1. Vegetation succession from ʻōhiʻa to hala can be observed today on old lava flows near the coast in Puna on Hawaiʻi Island.

2. Hawaiians may have taken advantage of this property of *Pandanus* leaves in the implementation of the pā hala method of kalo propagation practiced in Puna, Hawaiʻi, in which kalo was planted within intact hala groves, and branches and leaves were then cut to cover the growing taro (kalo) plants. The leaves were subsequently burned to provide nutrients for the kalo (Handy, Handy, & Pukui, 1972, pp. 104–105).

3. It is unclear how hala reached so far inland. Perhaps now-extinct large flightless birds or other unknown animals were responsible, although a slow progression inland without animal seed dispersers or the action of tsunami waves is possible.

4. The author lived for two years on Onotoa Island in the Republic of Kiribati in a large house constructed from *Pandanus* stem posts and *Pandanus* leaf thatch. The wall siding and lashing used to connect everything was made from coconut leaves and coconut fruit fiber. Large, culturally important meeting houses known as maneaba are also made primarily from *Pandanus* (Maude, 1980).

5. On the atolls of the central Pacific, *Pandanus* fruits are eaten raw or processed into several products, some of which can be stored for years to be eaten in case of food shortage or taken on long-duration voyages. In Kiribati, these preserved forms are still routinely given to friends and family who are leaving the islands for a long trip abroad.

BIBLIOGRAPHY

Ash, J. (1987). Demography, dispersal and production of *Pandanus tectorius* (Pandanaceae) in Fiji. *Australian Journal of Botany, 35*(3), 313–330.

Athens, J. S., & Ward, J. V. (1991). *Paleoenvironmental and archaeological investigations, Kawainui Marsh Flood Control Project, Oʻahu Island, Hawaiʻi.* Technical report. Honolulu: International Archaeological Research Institute.

Athens, J. S., & Ward, J. V. (1993). Environmental change and prehistoric Polynesian settlement in Hawaiʻi. *Asian Perspectives, 32,* 205–223.

Atkinson, I. A. E. (1970). Successional trends in the coastal and lowland forest of Mauna Loa and Kilauea volcanoes, Hawaiʻi. *Pacific Science, 24*(3), 387–400.

Balter, M. (2010). Beyond Kon-Tiki: Did Polynesians sail to South America? *Science, 328,* 1344–1347.

Bates, G. W. (1854). *Sandwich Island notes.* New York: Harper and Brothers.

Bennett, D. (2000). Preliminary survey and status report for *Varanus olivaceus* on Polillo Island. In D. Bennett (Ed.), *Wildlife of Polillo Island, Philippines.* Glossop, U.K.: Viper Press.

Bille, S. (1852). *Bericht Uber die Reise der Corvette Galathea um die Welt in den Jahren 1845, 46 und 47* (Vol. 2). Copenhagen: C. A. Reitzel, C. B. Lorck.

Bingham, H. (1849). *A residence of twenty-one years in the Sandwich Islands; or, The civil, religious, and political history of those islands: Comprising a particular view of the mission-ary operations connected with the introduction and progress of Christianity and civilization among the Hawaiian people.* Hartford, NY: H. Huntington, S. Converse.

Brigham, W. T. (1906). *Mat and basket weaving of the ancient Hawaiians described and com-pared with the basketry of the other Pacific Islanders* (Vol. 2). Honolulu: Bishop Museum Press.

Bryan, W. A. (1915). *Natural history of Hawai'i: Being an account of the Hawaiian people, the geology and geography of the islands, and the native and introduced plants and animals of the group.* Honolulu: Hawaiian Gazette.

Burney, D. A., James, H. F., Burney, L. P., Olson, S. L., Kikuchi, W., Wagner, W. L., et al. (2001). Fossil evidence for a diverse biota from Kaua'i and its transformation since human arrival. *Ecological Monographs, 71*(4), 615–641.

County of Los Angeles. (2004). *Los Angeles County 2004 agricultural crop report.* Arcadia, CA: Author.

Cox, P. A. (1985). Islands and dioecism: Insights from the reproductive ecology of *Pan-danus tectorius* in Polynesia. In J. White (Ed.), *Studies of plant demography: A festschrift for John L. Harper* (pp. 359–372). London: Academic Press.

Cox, P. A. (1990). Pollination and the evolution of breeding systems in Pandanaceae. *Annals of the Missouri Botanical Garden, 77,* 816–840.

Cunningham, J. (1994). Fossil discovery proves Stone's theory is correct. *Iridos* (Summer), 3.

Daly, C., & Halbleib, M. (2006). *Pacifc Islands (Hawai'i) average monthly and annual mini-mum and maximum temperature and mean dewpoint temperature, 1971–2000.* The PRISM Group at Oregon State University.

Davis, R. G. (1866). *Report of a portion of the decisions rendered by the Supreme Court of the Hawaiian Islands, in law, equity, admirality and probate 1857–1865* (Vol. 2). Honolulu: Government Press.

Devaney, D. M., Kelly, M., Lee, P. J., & Motteler, L. (1982). *Kaneohe: A history of change.* Honolulu: Bess Press.

Englberger, L., Aalbersberg, W., Dolodolotawake, U., Schierle, J., Humphries, J., Iuta, T., et al. (2007). Carotenoid content of *Pandanus* fruit cultivars and other foods of the Republic of Kiribati. *Public Health Nutrition, 9*(5), 631–643.

Englberger, L., Aalbersberg, W., Fitzgerald, M. H., Marks, G. C., & Chand, K. (2003). Provitamin A carotenoid content of different cultivars of edible *Pandanus* fruit. *Journal of Food Composition and Analysis, 16*(2), 237–247.

Fall, P. L. (2005). Vegetation change in the coastal-lowland rainforest at Avaiʻoʻvuna Swamp, Vavaʻu, Kingdom of Tonga. *Quaternary Research, 64*(3), 451–459.

Gaulke, M. (2010). Overview on the present knowledge on *Varanus mabitang* Gaulke and Curio, 2001, including new morphological and meristic data. *Biawak, 4*(2), 50–58.

Giambelluca, T. W., Chen, Q., Frazier, A. G., Price, J. P., Chen, Y.-L., Chu, P.-S. Eischeid, J. K., & Delparte, D. M. (2013). Online rainfall atlas of Hawaiʻi. *Bulletin of the American Meteorological Society, 94*, 313–316.

Gon, S. M., Allison, A., Cannarella, R. J., Jacobi, J. D., Kaneshiro, K. Y., Kido, M. H., et al. (2006). *A GAP analysis of Hawaiʻi: Final report.* Washington, DC: U.S. Department of the Interior, U.S. Geological Survey.

Guppy, H. (1906). *Observations of a naturalist in the Pacific between 1896 and 1899: Plant-dispersal* (Vol. 2). London: Macmillan.

Haddon, A. C., & Hornell, J. (1936). *Canoes of Oceania, volume I: The canoes of Polynesia, Fiji, and Micronesia.* Honolulu: Bishop Museum Press.

Handy, E. S. C., Handy, E. G., & Pukui, M. K. (1972). *Native planters in old Hawaiʻi: Their life, lore, and environment.* Honolulu: Bishop Museum Press.

Hotchkiss, S., & Juvik, J. O. (1999). A Late-Quaternary pollen record from Kaʻau Crater, Oʻahu, Hawaiʻi. *Quaternary Research, 52*(1), 115–128.

Hyndman, D. C. (1984). Ethnobotany of Wopkaimin *Pandanus:* Significant Papua New Guinea plant resource. *Economic Botany, 38*(3), 287–303.

Jones, T. L., Matisoo-Smith, E. A., & Ramirez-Aliaga, J. M. (2011). *Polynesians in America: Pre-Columbian contacts with the New World.* Lanham, MD: AltaMira Press.

Kamakau, S. M. (1961). *Ruling chiefs of Hawaiʻi.* Honolulu: Kamehameha Schools Press.

Kaufman, A., & Gallaher, T. (2011). *Effectiveness of vegetation for mitigating the coastal impact due to storm surge and tsunamis.* Honolulu: University of Hawaiʻi at Mānoa, Department of Tropical Plant and Soil Sciences.

Kirch, P. V. (1996). Late Holocene human-induced modifications to a central Polynesian island ecosystem. *Proceedings of the National Academy of Sciences, 93*(11), 5296–5300.

Krajina, V. J., Rock, J. F., & St. John, H. (1962). *Campus trees and plants.* Honolulu: University of Hawaiʻi at Mānoa.

Kumar, D., Kumar, S., Kumar, S., Singh, J., Sharma, C., & Aneja, K. R. (2010). Antimicrobial and preliminary phytochemical screening of crude leaf extract of *Pandanus odoratissimus* L. *Pharmacology Online, 2*, 600–610.

Kvacek, J., & Herman, A. B. (2004). Monocotyledons from the Early Campanian (Cretaceous) of Grünbach, Lower Austria. *Review of Palaeobotany and Palynology, 128*(3–4), 323–353.

Ladefoged, T. N., Kirch, P. V., Gon III, S. M., Chadwick, O. A., Hartshorn, A. S., & Vitousek, P. M. (2009). Opportunities and constraints for intensive agriculture in the Hawaiian archipelago prior to European contact. *Journal of Archaeological Science, 36*(10), 2374–2383.

Lee, M. A. B. (1985). The dispersal of *Pandanus tectorius* by the land crab *Cardisoma carnifex. Oikos, 45*(2), 169–173.

Londonkar, R., & Kamble, A. (2009). Evaluation of free radical scavenging activity of *Pandanus odoratissimus. International Journal of Pharmacology, 5,* 377–380.

Maude, H. E. (1980). *The Gilbertese Maneaba.* Suva: Institute of Pacific Studies and Kiribati Extention Center of the University of the South Pacific.

Meilleur, B. A., Maigret, M. A., & Manshardt, R. (1997). *Hala and wauke in Hawai'i.* Honolulu: Bishop Museum Press.

Nakanishi, H. (1988). Dispersal ecology of the maritime plants in the Ryukyu Islands, Japan. *Ecological Research, 3*(2), 163–173.

Nandasena, N. A. K., Tanaka, N., & Tanimoto, K. (2008). Tsunami current inundation of ground with coastal vegetation effects: An initial step towards a natural solution for tsunami amelioration. *Journal of Earthquake and Tsunami, 2*(2), 151–171.

Prebble, A., & Dowe, J. L. (2008). The late Quaternary decline and extinction of palms on oceanic Pacific islands. *Quaternary Science Reviews, 27,* 2546–2567.

Shepard, F. P., MacDonald, G. A., & Cox, D. C. (1950). *The tsunami of April 1, 1946.* Berkeley: Scripps Institution of Oceanography of the University of California.

Starr, F., Starr, K., & Wood, K. (2006). *Maui offshore islets botanical survey.* Maui: Department of Land and Natural Resources, Division of Forestry and Wildlife and Offshore Islet Restoration Committee.

Sterling, E. P., & Summers, C. C. (1978). *Sites of O'ahu.* Honolulu: Bishop Museum Press.

Stickney, F. S. (1934). *The external anatomy of the red date scale, Phoenicococcus marlatti Cockerell, and its allies.* Washington, DC: U.S. Department of Agriculture.

Summerhayes, G. R., Leavesley, M., Fairbairn, A., Mandui, H., Field, J., Ford, A., et al. (2010). Human adaptation and plant use in highland New Guinea 49,000 to 44,000 years ago. *Science, 330,* 78–81.

Summers, C. C. (1990). *Hawaiian cordage.* Honolulu: Bishop Museum Press.

Teng, L. C., Shen, T. C., & Goh, S. H. (1979). The flavoring compound of the leaves of *Pandanus amaryllifolius. Economic Botany, 33*(1), 72–74.

Thaman, R. R. (1992). Batiri kei Baravi: The ethnobotany of Pacific Island coastal plants. *Atoll Research Bulletin, 361,* 1–62.

Thrum, T. G. (1900). *Hawaiian almanac and annual for 1901.* Honolulu: Thos. G. Thrum.

Wagner, W. L., Herbst, D. R., & Sohmer, S. H. (1999). *Manual of the flowering plants of Hawai'i* (Vols. 1–2). Honolulu: University of Hawai'i and Bishop Museum Press.

Whittaker, R. J., Bush, M. B., & Richards, K. (1989). Plant recolonization and vegetation succession on the Krakatau Islands, Indonesia. *Ecological Monographs, 59*(2), 59–123.

Wiles, G. J., Engbring, J., & Falanruw, M. V. C. (1991). Population status and natural history of *Pteropus mariannus* on Ulithi Atoll, Caroline Islands. *Pacific Science, 45*(1), 76–84.

Wilkes, C. (1845). *Narrative of the United States Exploring Expedition during the years 1838, 1839, 1840, 1841, 1842* (Vol. 4). London: Wiley and Putnam.

Yen, D. E. (1993). The origins of subsistence agriculture in Oceania and the potentials for future tropical food crops. *Economic Botany, 47*(1), 3–14.

A Conversation with Uncle Roy L. Benham

Prepared by *Kaiwipunikauikawēkiu Lipe*

E ka mea heluhelu, aloha nui kāua! For each volume of the Hawaiʻinuiākea monograph series, I have had the privilege of talking story with an amazing contributing member of our community. This time, I had the honor of learning with Uncle Roy Benham, kūpuna and well-known maker of lei hala. It is most appropriate to highlight his moʻolelo in this edition focused on hala because of the rare cut he makes on the hala keys, which he continues today at the young age of eighty-nine! We see his beautiful lei adorning folks around the island and yet so few of us know how he makes them.

The setting of this particular interview is important to the context of the moʻolelo we share. Uncle Roy came to meet with me at Bishop Museum on the same day that several of the authors of this volume were also meeting (Betty Kam, Dr. Ipolani Wong, Dr. Lia Keawe, Marques Marzan, and Tim Gallaher). Consequently, we were all in the room when he decided to share his moʻolelo and demonstrate his art. In his kūpuna style, he kindly and firmly invited all of us to gather round and pay attention. We were all invited to ask questions and enjoy this time with him while he shared with us his craft. Our questions encouraged Uncle Roy to reflect on his art and to tell some very interesting tales. It was treasured time for all of us to spend with Uncle Roy. He shared so generously and was ever so patient with us.

Dear reader, some of you may have difficulty reading this text, but I hope you will persevere. A lesson we learned from our time with Uncle Roy is the importance of haʻi moʻolelo. Uncle Roy so perfectly demonstrates to us here that as moʻolelo are told, one story reminds us of another story, sometimes of the past and sometimes of the future. Therefore, the transcript below is not presented chronologically or thematically. Instead, it is presented as Uncle Roy told it so that you, the reader, may enjoy not only his manaʻo about hala but also his classic kūpuna style of haʻi moʻolelo. I encourage you to read it from beginning to end, as there are many treasures within.

Punihei: Uncle, I was thinking about you the other day because I was on Maunakea Street and I saw these leis but the hala was cut really short and square and I thought, Oh! So different!

Uncle Roy: Yeah, that's how they cut it. By the way, I challenge you . . . there's no "s" in Hawaiian.

Punihei: Yes, you're right. Hala leis. You're right.

Uncle Roy: You know what the "s" is? N-A. Nā.

Punihei: Yes, nā hala, nā lei. You're absolutely correct. Mahalo for that.

Uncle Roy: It's a real challenge, but I've got so that I'm aware now. [To all the people in the room] Can I talk to you all one time? Let me do what I do when I demonstrate this in various places downtown. I show the children that the hala is used primarily for its leaves. The yellow that I picked is too ripe. I tell them that the hala is the fruit of the tree, but it's more known for its leaves, lau hala. And then I tell them that the Hawaiian word for "leaf" is "lau." And then I tell them that the noun comes first in Hawaiian and then the adjective. Then I ask them, "How do you say coconut in Hawaiian?" None of them remember. Then I say, "Oh it's the little neighborhood on the way to Hawai'i Kai." Then they say, "Oh, Niu Valley!" Then I say, "So how do you say coconut leaf?" And 75 percent of them say, "Lau niu." "Eh! Too good you! Not niu lau."

But your question on how do I know when it's ripe. Well this is green and there's no space between the keys; it's all tight. Then the riper it gets the bigger the space gets. Like this one is kind of big. . . . This is about two weeks ago, no, a week ago. The space gets bigger to the point and as it gets bigger the color moves up. So at a certain point and time you can see the color. But if you can see it really good it's too ripe and it begins to fall and you can't use it for a lei. It gets too soft. This one is a little too ripe. So what I do is I take one of these [the fruit] . . . and as I say the aphids are everywhere and I have to wipe them all off. . . . I usually wipe them off with a rag.

Punihei: Uncle, what are the aphids?

Uncle Roy: The white bugs. They are on everything. See that white stuff? And where there are aphids there are ants. The ants are in there too. They crawl all the way up the tree. What I do is this first [cut the bottom of the key into a little point]. Each one. [As Uncle Roy begins to demonstrate his cut, he happens on an overripe key.] Now this one is too ripe already. . . . Can't do it, I don't think. It's beginning to crack. Yeah, it is too soft. You see, it is no good. It is too soft and it falls apart. But the smell is there. Try smell that. When it is really ripe it has a terrific odor. The women are the ones who like the smell. When it's ripe it's really a strong odor.

Punihei: Oooh . . . it smells like perfume.

Uncle Roy: Here's my red tree [shows a red lei].

Group: Wow!

Uncle Roy: Sometimes . . . see, the mildew gets on it. But sometimes the keys sit together like that. You know on the red tree, sometimes people ask, "Where do

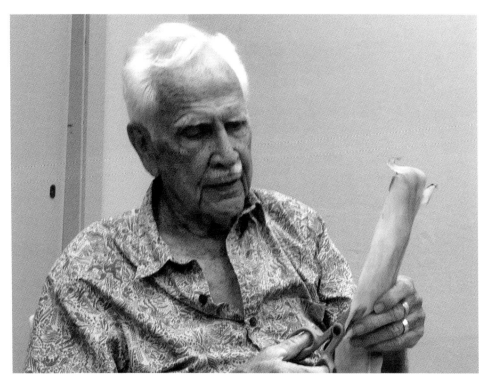
Uncle Roy Benham. Image courtesy of author.

Various colors of the hala fruit. Image courtesy of author.

Uncle Roy demonstrating the Hāna cut. Image courtesy of author.

Uncle Roy's lei hala. Image courtesy of author.

Uncle Roy's finishing touch: a ti-leaf bow. Image courtesy of author.

you get the red tree? Where do you get the red ones from?" And I say, "From the tree." There's red, yellow, and orange.

Punihei: Uncle, do you grow your own?

Uncle Roy: No, no.

Lia: You have your secret stash all around!

Uncle Roy: Oh yeah. I know where all the trees are. And you know, people plant this tree for basically two reasons. One, it's a nonrubbish tree. The leaves are big when they dry, easy to clean, and [they] don't have to worry about leaves falling down like the monkey pod and stuff. And the other one is that it has thorns and the tree trunk has thorns, so that means there won't be any children climbing the trees. Don't have to worry about children climbing the trees.

When I see a tree that has ripe ones that I want, I go knock on the door and ask the people if I can have their fruit. They say, "Oh, sure. You like the fruit? Go, take 'em!" Because when this falls down and it gets real ripe, it attracts flies. The flies come because it is soft and pulpy. So people say, "Take 'em! Take 'em!"

Punihei: So Uncle, you pick 'em when it's not ripe and let it ripen?

Uncle Roy: No, no. I pick it when it is ripe. This one I picked just on my way here at Kaumakapili Church. There's enough space in there [between the keys of the fruit] so you can at least see a little bit of yellow. What I use is a screwdriver to get the first key out. Once you get a few out, then they pop out okay. See, this one is kind of yellow already.

Betty: It gets darker as it gets older?

Uncle Roy: Yeah. See, look the difference. When I was working—I was working as a civilian with the army—I got assigned to the Presidio in San Francisco, California. So, my wife and I moved up there. Then I got reassigned back to Fort Shafter and my wife didn't want to move [from San Francisco] with the two children. She wanted to wait till school ended up there and then come down, so, I came down and I was by myself here waiting for them. After work I didn't have much to do, you know? But Billie Fernandez's sister, Barbara I think her name was, had a floral shop at Koko Head by Punchbowl. So on my way home I would stop there in the afternoon and help her with flowers and make haku and lei and stuff and there was—[a pause and then looking at Betty] remember Charlie Davis?

Betty: Yes.

Uncle Roy: He had a brother, Francis Davis. Francis was helping Bobbie [Barbara] Fernandez, too. He was making hala lei and he showed me how to cut. 'Cause, you know, if you go down to Maunakea Street, what they do is they cut it about right there [three-quarters of the way down the key], square, sort of in blocks . . . just right below the hard part. You see, this is the hard part. I can't cut this. They figure out where the hard part is and they cut it right there. And of course they use the hala with the bigger fruit. With the bigger hala they get the longer piece. And then they sew it with laua'e in between.

But anyway, Francis Davis was showing Bobbie how he made hala, and he was cutting it like this . . . this way [a more diagonal cut]. And I asked him to show me how and he said he would. See, I do it like that so it fits better when I string it.

Punihei: Uncle, how long ago was that when you learned how to make lei?

Uncle Roy: About thirty years ago [pause], twenty-five years ago. And so he showed me how to do this and it took me a while before I learned how. Have you folks been to Hāna, Maui?

Group: 'Ae.

Uncle Roy: It is loaded with hala trees. And Francis called this the "Hāna cut."

Punihei: Oh, so this is the style from Hāna?

Uncle Roy: 'Cause Hāna has plenty trees. But after I cut it for a while, I called it the "hana-hana" cut! One time before I started doing this, my wife and I went on a trip to Maui. You know in Hāna they have state housing with the little cottages you could rent, and we rented one of the cottages, and it was in the middle of a hala grove. Holy mackerel! That's where I first got attracted to hala, you know?

When I was a kupuna in the elementary schools—I was a kupuna for eleven years—we had to do a lot of the studying of Hawaiian subjects. I read one article that was written in about 1921 or '22 and it was a guy that was visiting parts of this island [O'ahu], and he said he had been to Kahuku, and when he left Kahuku he was given a hala lei, and he said Kahuku was the land of the hala. Evidently that's what it was before the sugarcane came. And guess where I was born and raised?

Lia: Kahuku!

Uncle Roy: Kahuku. I get all chicken skin. When I read that, well, no wonder, you know? But when I was there [Kahuku] it was all sugarcane. Over by where the water station used to be is where the hala used to be. And if I'm not saying anything that's right, let me know, you know [directed at Tim, the botanist].

Tim: Everything you are saying is right.

Uncle Roy: I don't think the Hawaiians made these kinds of lei until after Captain Cook 'cause they didn't have this [pointing to the X-Acto knife]. The closest thing to this would be a sharp bamboo thing. When Captain Cook came, they [Hawaiians] saw two things that they wanted. One was knives and the other was the pot. Which reminds me—Hawaiians used this [hala keys] as a paintbrush. They used to paint their tapa—'cause you know the tapa colors were bright. When they wanted to make it darker, they took these [leaves on the hala fruit]—see, this one is just starting to brown. When it dries it gets dark brown. They took those dark brown leaves and put it in boiling water and then made it a stain.

I maintain that Hawaiians give this lei when you are starting a new phase of your life—going into a new phase—birthdays, graduations, promotions, if you move to a new house and have a housewarming. Politicians can wear it when they get elected. When Mufi Hanneman got elected, I gave him one like this. He said, "Oh! Terrific! How come you never gave me this kind when I was running?" I said, "'Cause you not there yet! Your life doesn't change till you get elected." "Oh okay, okay." And of course, people say that they see them use this at funerals. Well that's your biggest change. You going to the new life. In fact I know some Hawaiian families who put this in their burial casket. They are aware how the lei dries.

They dry like that [brings out a dried lei]. If I use the big one, they dry bigger. If I use the red, they dry darker. My friends who make hat lei out of that get a clear lacquer and they spray it. It does two things. It gives it a nice shine and it keeps the bugs off—'cause the bugs are gonna get in there. My friend Ainsley Halemanu, he gets yellow spray and red spray and he says it lasts forever. But that's phony, you know? [laughs]. Can't make a fake lei!

Betty: Can I ask you one thing? You said the leaves, you boiled the leaves?

Uncle Roy: Yeah, only these leaves, not the bigger leaves. Only the leaves from the fruit.

Betty: And you use that to darken the tapa?

Uncle Roy: No, you put it in the boiling water and it makes a stain . . . like a dyed stain. Yes [for tapa], and they used the hala brush and brushed the water on their tapa.

Betty: So it just darkens the tapa?

Uncle Roy: Yeah, it darkens the tapa.

Lia: Uncle, darkens the tapa or able to make design on the tapa?

Uncle Roy: No, no, just darkens. They still use their stamps. They never paint it.

Betty: That's a new thing for me because I've always thought the uncolored tapa, it's not white-white, but natural color. But now what I'm gonna look for are tapa that's not painted but colored this way.

Uncle Roy: Yeah, yeah. When it's part of their tapa that they wanted to make darker—maybe make a strip, too, and then after it's dried put the stamp on. By the way, that's how I got my Hawaiian name. When I was a kupuna [in the Department of Education] they taught us how to make tapa. We had wauke and we are pounding. For the first time in my life I was pounding wauke and making tapa. I was really impressed. Our leader asked one of the aunties to give me a Hawaiian name. My mother had five children. Three of them had Hawaiian names. Me and Clayton no more. Gun funnit! So our leader said, "You gotta give Uncle Roy one Hawaiian name." So this aunty, one day she said, "Okay, I got a Hawaiian name for you." "Well, what's the name?" She said, "Well, I was watching him making tapa and while he was pounding the tapa he was so impressed on how white the wauke gets." I said, "Look how bright this is get-ting!" Then it dries sort of tan, but while it's wet it's real bright. So she said, "He was talking about the brightness of the wauke and I looked at his light skin, 'Ilikea." So they gave me the name 'Ilikea [laughter].

Our elementary school teachers who have access to hala trees pick the dried key off the ground after they've fallen from the fruit core and give each child one. The child then scrapes off the dried pulp and ends up with a paintbrush. I did this as a student at Kahuku Elementary School.

One Hawaiian guy told me that when the Hawaiians found one that had real strong fiber, they jumped in the ocean and cleaned their teeth with salt water by dipping the brush in the ocean. Too good, eh?

Lia: Hoihoi!

Uncle Roy: A good idea. The next time I get in the ocean I gonna do that! Let's see. What else is there? Basically, that's what I tell the folks about this plant. The fact that it is more important for the leaves than the fruit. Oh, there's another thing. There's a male tree and a female tree and you can't tell the difference when they're small. The female tree has the fruit and the male tree has a yellow brush-like leaf that fertilizes the fruit. I lived in a condominium and I had room for one hala tree and I thought, "Ho! It would be good if I had one hala tree and it would be right there for me." So I got one hala tree, one red one from this guy I knew—he had a red tree. The thing was growing—it grew really good. It turned out to be male with the hinano flower. Oh shoot! You know what this Hawaiian guy told me, he said, "Who planted it?" I said, "I did." He said, "Next time tell your wife to plant it!" And same way if you go to the nursery, to buy it in a pot, can't tell which is which. There's no way to tell when they're small, yeah? [Tim agrees with Uncle Roy.]

Tim: When they're small, no.

Betty: So Uncle Roy, maybe this is not a smart question, but when do you think these kinds of lei started to be made?

Uncle Roy: I think after the native Hawaiians had access to metal knives. 'Cause I think the way they make it at Maunakea Street [square cut], they could do it easily enough.

Betty: Then they would string it with?

Uncle Roy: It's easy to poke something through it because you only going through this fiber. You can't poke anything through here [points at the nut]. There's a gal in my—who is a kupuna with us—I forget her name now. When you eighty-nine years old you forget names. But look. [Shows a lei made out of the nuts.]

Group: Wow! Oh my gosh! [General admiration.]

Uncle Roy: She decided to make a lei out of this. You see, on that one [hala nut lei], you have to wait until it gets dry. What she did is cut it down [takes one of the older keys] like this—'cause the dark shell is in there—and she sanded it on a sander to get the dark color. And then when you are pau you gotta drill the hole, yeah?

Betty: So when tourism came about in the '20s and '30s, that's when lei started getting really popular. Were these [hala lei] popular, too?

Uncle Roy: I don't think so. 'Cause, number one, they weren't fragrant. If they were fragrant you couldn't make the lei because it was too soft. So I don't think it was popular. I think it was just colorful.

Betty: Did you ever make other kinds of lei?

Uncle Roy: Yeah, I do. I make lei poʻo and lei ʻāʻī with the haku method. In fact, I decided when my grandson was growing up and needed more money—my wife and I raised our grandson—I used to go to University of Hawaiʻi graduation and sell all the lei. So I got to know all the lei sellers and then one year the school, the university, decided they were gonna charge all the lei sellers for space and so I organized a couple of them and we went to see the dean and we talked them out of it. I said, "You know, this is a Hawaiian custom and they've been doing this for years. You can't charge them to sell lei and stuff." So they called it off. They were a good group.

Lia: Uncle, what do you use to string the hala?

Uncle Roy: Crochet thread.

Punihei: And do you use a lei needle?

Uncle Roy: Yes, I use a lei needle but I cut it short. And it is getting hard to find lei needles now. Here's the kind I bought not too long ago. Look how skinny that is! But I like to use this one [shows a thicker needle]. Then I just hook it on, make it double length, and then string it. It goes through the stuff easy.

Betty: You are known for your hala lei. Do you make many?

Uncle Roy: Eh, I put my grandson through college with this. I paid his tuition. He would say, "Eh Grandpa, sell plenty, Grandpa!"

Betty: Really! That's amazing!

Uncle Roy: I've shown people how to do this. There's one guy who is doing it and occasionally I'll see one of his lei. I'm glad he's doing it.

Tim: Uncle, do you find fruit year round?

Uncle Roy: Yeah. That's another thing. There's a saying, "When the hala is ripe, the wana is fat." And I told this guy, "Eh! I can find hala year-round. That means the wana is fat all year-round." And he said, "No, no, no. The wana by that tree is fat." Yeah, that's right. 'Cause the trees in Hawaiʻi Kai, sometimes they're ripe over here, but the trees in Kailua, they're not ripe. And they don't all get ripe the same time. It depends on when you plant it.

Punihei: Uncle, did you ever teach the kids in school about making hala lei?

Uncle Roy: Yeah. I would just show them how to cut and I would just tell them when you grow up and get older, 'cause this was elementary children, maybe they can cut like this. And then I show them how they cut on Maunakea Street.

Betty: Uncle Roy, you've been a teacher for many years. Who do you consider your greatest teacher?

Uncle Roy: I think my Hawaiian teacher, Don Mitchell. He was my science teacher at Kamehameha when I was a student. One of the things he did, I'll never forget—the girls' school had moved. We were over here [Bishop Museum]. This was our campus. And right where the auditorium is, the old school auditorium up on the hill [Waonahele]. He started a Hawaiian garden there. I don't think that thing is still going, is it?

Lia: It's all cement now.

Uncle Roy: Oh, shoot. And he tried to plant all the native Hawaiian plants. Preserve. It was such a terrific idea. And in his science class we would go on a bus and go up and he'd show us all the native plants. It was really terrific.

Lia: Uncle, when you went back to teach at Kamehameha, what did you teach?

Uncle Roy: I taught art for all the classes and I taught American history in the eighth grade. From seventh, eighth, and ninth grade, art was a requirement. Tenth, eleventh, and twelfth it was elective.

Punihei: What kind of art did you teach, Uncle?

Uncle Roy: I taught mostly painting. Watercolor painting, drawing, freelance drawing. I was an art major at the University of California. When I was about to graduate, I wrote to the school. Al Bailey was the principal—and asked him if they had a job for me 'cause I would like to come teach at Kamehameha. He told me the story after that—when he got my letter he went to the art teacher, Myron Stout was his name, and he said, "Eh, one of your students wants to come up here and teach." And Myron said, "You know, I've been here for about twelve years and I never did take sabbatical. Let me take my sabbatical and he can come." And that's what happened. He took his sabbatical so I came and took his place. And he was my art teacher. And of course, once he went on sabbatical he started painting and he said, " 'Nuff teaching already!" So he never did come back. But I only stayed there seven years. My hair turned white—I quit.

Betty: So Uncle, did you ever weave [lau hala]?

Uncle Roy: Yeah, I made that [points to a small lau hala pouch]. When we were kūpuna [in the Department of Education] they showed us how. But I forget now. I use it [the lau hala pouch] for my cards. Look, I made my own business cards.

Betty: Too good! You used address labels!

Uncle Roy: You know I don't have my own computer. Anybody want one [a business card]?

Punihei: I think we all want one! So Uncle, when you sell lei, do you sell it directly to people or do you sell to Maunakea Street?

Uncle Roy: No, no. Directly to people. I sell them for twenty [dollars].

Punihei: Uncle, I know you said there was one guy you taught how to make lei hala but are there others?

Uncle Roy: I don't know where he operates from. But I've seen people with the lei and I know it's the guy I taught, but I don't know how or where he does it. I don't even know his name. I guess I should find out. Next time I see a lei that I didn't make, I'm gonna say, "Who made this for you?"

Betty: [Returning to Uncle Roy's lei] So this is the Hāna style?

Uncle Roy: Francis Davis called it the Hāna cut. I just called it the hana-hana cut.

Punihei: Who did Francis Davis learn from?

Uncle Roy: Well, he was from Hale'iwa. Their family had plenty hala there. Waialua has plenty hala. I don't know. I guess he learned from his family. I didn't ask him.

Punihei: Did you teach any of your kids how to make lei hala?

Uncle Roy: My children? I have two daughters. One is in Idaho and one is in Tennessee.

Punihei: Oh, not too much hala over there.

Uncle Roy: My grandson is in Santa Cruz. So I live in Hawai'i Kai retirement community. Somebody said, "So how do you like that place?" I said, "It's okay but got plenty older people." [Group laughs.]

Betty: When you were teaching at Kamehameha, did you teach students how to do any crafts besides art?

Uncle Roy: See, we had a shop. Each student had to take shop. We had shop— carpenter shop, welding shop, and agriculture shop. So they had that kind of making things experiences. I didn't do much of that.

Punihei: Uncle, which part [of the hala] do you eat?

Tim: Oh yeah. In Micronesia they would eat this part [points to the pulp of the key]. Some are fibrous. But the ones that they have, have been selected over a long time so that there are hardly any fibers in them. It is just like biting into a fruit. Like an apple. For the longest time, it was thought to be a different species altogether because the fruit is that big [indicating a length nearly as long as his hand]. It's sweet and fleshy.

Uncle Roy: Have you ever seen any that big?

Tim: I have.

Uncle Roy: Holy moly. The keys must be big.

Tim: They are. They are like the size of your hand. And from what I understand, some of the Micronesians and Marshallese have brought them [to Hawai'i] so they are growing in people's yards. But I've not seen one yet here.

Uncle Roy: See, with this one [the Hawaiian hala], when it got real ripe, you could bite it and pull it through your teeth like artichoke. The pulpy part. What about the leaves [of the Micronesian hala]? Are they wider?

Tim: The leaves are very similar to ours. In the Gilbert Islands, they have 200 named varieties of hala.

Uncle Roy: Holy mackerel!

Tim: And some of them are for the fruit, some of them are for the leaves, and some of them are actually for the stem. Like the house I lived in was almost 100 percent hala.

Punihei: What is their name for hala?

Tim: The tree is "te kaina." And the fruit is "te tou." I can't remember the name of the leaf. Different names for each part.

Uncle Roy: Yeah, that's right. The Hawaiians use the tree trunk in their house building.

Punihei: Do they weave? Like we do?

Tim: Oh yeah. But I would say they don't focus on high-quality, fine things. Because they are living a subsistence lifestyle.

Uncle Roy: I think it has been shown that Hawaiians were the most skillful in weaving the hala.

Punihei: Uncle, is it only you or are there other kūpuna who are making this kind of lei now?

Uncle Roy: I don't know anyone. The one that I taught, the younger ones. The older ones don't want to. This is my therapy. It keeps me busy. I go around and cut hala and stuff. Like when I was cutting this one today [at Kaumakapili Church], one of the workers in the church came and we talked story and got to know each other better. Every now and then I take one of their hala and make a lei and put [it] on the altar.

Punihei: Uncle, do you teach hala classes? How to make lei?

Uncle Roy: I did several times. I think I did one in Hawaiʻi Kai. And I did one at Central YMCA by the ʻIolani Palace. But they come and they see me doing this and they try about two or three sessions and they say, "Pau already. I tired." They think it's too complicated. You know I told them many times, "You not going to be successful at first. You just gotta keep going at it until you get the feel of it . . . how hard to cut and how hard to press and eventually you get it." But a lot of them didn't want to go through all of that.

Punihei: So if people want to learn, do they just call you up?

Uncle Roy: Well, I've been going to Native Hawaiian Books and Things. I've been there a few times and people see me. And whenever I go and demonstrate anywhere, some of them will come up and say, "Can we get together later on?" Something like that.

Betty: Thank you for teaching us. Now I know the Hāna cut.

Punihei: It's hard, though. He makes it look so easy! I watched you do it one time and I went home and showed my husband and I thought, "Oh my gosh! I'm gonna cut my finger off. I better stop now!"

Uncle Roy: You see, the thing is, don't forget, I'm pointing down all the time. My blade is down. Even when I do the bridge thing, I'm going down. You gotta watch it. I'm going down and I'm turning my blade in. I turn my blade in to go around that shell. Then you have to watch this side. See, when you are cutting, you only go down and as far as the first cut. And then you watch you don't go down too far. And then you go down to the next one. Now look, sometimes you come to a place where there is no ridge.

Let me show you where there's no ridge. I take my scissors and I make a ridge. 'Cause on some of them there's a big flat area with no ridge and I just cut it with a scissors and make a ridge.

Marques: Uncle, how long does it take you to make one lei?

Uncle Roy: If I don't wala'au, about forty-five minutes.

Lia: How many lei can you make with that fruit?

Uncle Roy: About two, two and a half.

Betty: About forty key?

Uncle Roy: And if you get the big kind, the long kind, you don't have to cut as many. This one I need about forty-five or fifty [keys]. But the big ones, only about thirty-five.

Marques: How long with wala'au?

Uncle Roy: When I'm at Native Hawaiian Books and Things and the tourist come by, takes long time.

Tim: Uncle, is there any significance to the various colors? Or is it just what people prefer?

Uncle Roy: It is just what people prefer. But it seems everyone prefers the red. As soon as I have a red one they buy 'em right away.

Marques: How many lei do you usually make in a week?

Uncle Roy: Oh plenty. It depends on how many orders. I make five or six a week. Just to have them.

Punihei: How do you store these if you want to keep the color before it goes dry?

Uncle Roy: In a Ziploc bag, in the refrigerator. See, this one I made with three colors. See, I can wear 'em for about two or three weeks and then I don't want to wear it anymore and I hang it on the picture.

When my wife passed away I made a nice red one for her. And I had it on her picture at the services. And once we buried her ashes I took the lei and I put it on the picture in the house. And it is still hanging there. Eight years ago and it still hanging on her picture. I sprayed it, though.

Betty: And this is an original bow [ti-leaf bow on the lei]. I never saw anybody make this kind of bow.

Uncle Roy: Take the ti-leaf. Then you split it. 'Cause I don't go store and buy ribbons. Get rid of the brown edge [of the ti-leaf]. [Uncle Roy proceeds to make a bow.]

Betty: This is a Benham original!

Lia: Nani. That's so pretty! All homemade. Uncle, you have to know, the work that you do, you are a treasure.

Punihei: Thank you, Uncle Roy.

After we finished the formal interview and I turned the recorder off, I sat with Uncle Roy and we ate lunch together. We continued to talk story about hala and also about his wife, whom he had mentioned several times throughout his moʻolelo. In those few moments as he spoke about her, described her beauty, and told me how much he missed her, it became clear to me that making lei hala has always been about deep aloha. He first became attracted to hala while with his beloved wife in Hāna, learned the Hāna cut while passing time until his ʻohana came home from California, made lei to help fund his grandson's college education, and now continues his craft in fond memory of his wife. His stories reminded me of something my kumu hula always points out, which is to always make lei with goodness and aloha in your naʻau. Mahalo Uncle Roy for demonstrating the art of not only making lei hala but also of doing things from a place of profound aloha. This is truly a most important lesson that should never be forgotten. Through work like making lei, this lesson can be instilled in our keiki and our moʻopuna so that aloha may always continue.

The Lauhala Mat

Jenna Robinson

I wrote and presented this piece at the spring 2012 graduation ceremony at the University of Hawaiʻi at Mānoa. The weaving of a lauhala mat reflects the sum of my experiences as a university student. I believe that all of us are unique leaves, growing and weaving together. With each day we become more intertwined, more invested in each other's future even as our collective purpose as a community is apparent. Our individual talents and beauty contribute to the strength of the mat that in turn supports us as individuals. I also wanted this poem to highlight the beauty of Hawaiian culture, which enriches anyone's life if they are open and sensitive to what these legendary islands and native people have to offer.

We each arrived on this campus
as different leaves from different trees,
knowing nothing deeper than our own wants and needs.
Freshmen socially relentless, absorbed in
the present tense, searching for that
illustrious aloha to replace the love we
left.
Little did those leaves know how
we would grow
into a strong, beautiful lauhala mat.
Each woman and man become
interlocking strands holding each
other together to create something
better than us alone.
So we weave. As
freshmen
trying to figure out a balance
between sleeping, partying, passing
classes
and juggling finances.
A system that we never really do figure out. But how

come no one ever warned me about the struggle as a
human being,
constantly searching for meaning.
As you are pushed to intellectual limitations, you
stumble across the greatest study buddy, who has all the
answers to every test in biology
in exchange for an attentive ear to clear their mind, which, of
course, you happily provide.

We weave.

As sophomores floating in
intellectual limbo, lost for direction.
Sometimes struck with crisis and trauma.
On the verge of life and death, craving
greater purpose.
The moment you lose hope
an unlikely friend lends down a rope,
reminding you to look into your heart and
relocate your art for life
as a strand in the mat of an aliʻi
lining up the mountain path for chiefly procession.
Never before had you realized the real lessons are the
ones you learn outside of class.

one strand two
up over and through, We
weave.

as juniors
21 young and fun.
No longer knowing the days of week
but places and spaces for the best happy hours
to release from overwhelming internships and jobs
and thoughts of dropout classmates who reluctantly became moms.
Somehow you survived this long and
continue to push on.
All of a sudden things start to click
awakened to your niche. Friends become
coworkers, teachers become peers.

You overcome fears and faults to
become a unique adult. Bold.
Cause you know,
no one else has the skills you hold.

one strand two
strands three
united we
continue to weave.

as seniors developing
ulcers
stressing over post-graduation plans and
hands
that never seem to cease typing papers. Wondering
if the "real world" is any greater than the reality you
have grown to know
and whether there is anyplace in the world for the love that has
taken you so long to show.
After today you go out into a new domain,
apprehensive yet willing.
Although you are connected to all the souls surrounding you please
remember:
'A'ohe hala 'ula i ka po.
No hala fruit shows its color in the darkness of night.
No one can appreciate your inner light

if you do not let it shine. Beauty must be
seen to be enjoyed.

We will never cease to weave.

One thing is for certain
I leave my undergraduate years at UH a better person because I no longer
see myself as an island alone in the Pacific. I wake up each morning on
this blessed life bestowing rock shocked that I am intertwined with such
talented people.
I am not Hawaiian,
I was not born in Hawai'i, but
this is my home.

You have all become my family.
Just like a lauhala mat unified
through our diversity,
we have become a powerful united entity.

Contributors

C. Kurt Dewhurst serves as the director of arts and cultural initiatives and senior fellow, University Outreach and Engagement; director emeritus and curator of folklife and cultural heritage at the Michigan State University Museum; and professor of English at Michigan State University. A founder of the folk and traditional arts programs at the museum, he coordinates a variety of state, national, and international folklife research, collection development, and community engagement programs. His research interests include folk arts, material culture, ethnicity, occupational folk culture, cultural economic development, and cultural heritage policy. As a professor in the English Department at MSU, he teaches courses in folklife, material folk culture, and museum studies. He currently serves as chairperson of the board of trustees for the American Folklife Center of the Library of Congress and is past president of the American Folklore Society. He was honored with the 2004 Américo Paredes prize by the American Folklore Society for excellence in integrating scholarship with engagement with communities. He has led or co-led many local, state, and national research, publication, exhibition, education, festival program, and arts service projects focused on Native arts.

Timothy Gallaher is a botanist specializing in the coastal ecosystems of Hawai'i and the tropical Indo-Pacific. Born and raised in Hawai'i, he became interested in hala (pandanus) as a Peace Corps volunteer in the Republic of Kiribati, where the fruit is an important staple food and continues to be an important part of the material culture. He earned his PhD at the University of Hawai'i at Mānoa in 2013. The topic of his dissertation was the evolutionary and biogeographic history of pandanus. He and his wife have two children.

Betty Lou Kam, now the Princess Bernice Pauahi Bishop Museum's director of cultural collections, has been a museum professional for over three decades and has been involved in many aspects and roles during this time. Her tenure at the Bishop Museum began in 1980 as collection manager of the museum's historic photographs under the supervision and tutelage of photo historian Lynn A. Davis. This astounding collection of a million images of Hawai'i and the Pacific was inspiring and provided a good foundation for instruction and development. During her employment at the museum, Ms. Kam has served as chairman of the library and archives, collections manager of the anthropology collection, and vice president for cultural resources. She has also managed specific projects that span a range of topics and purposes, including contracts for the development of Hawaiian kapa designs for major airports in the state, a series of Hawaiian music and dance programs that spotlighted important kumu hula, database conversions, and a remarkable photograph documentation project that involved interviewing and collecting data from seniors in ʻŌlaʻa, Hawaiʻi Island. An exciting role and responsibility has been the development of exhibitions at the Bishop Museum and work in traveling exhibits with venues outside Hawaiʻi. Ms. Kam was raised in Kāneʻohe and attended the University of Hawaiʻi at Mānoa. She serves on the Hawaiʻi State Board of Geographic Names and as a commissioner for the Mayor's Office on Culture and the Arts.

Lia OʻNeill M. A. Keawe was born on Oʻahu and raised on Hawaiʻi Island in Hilo. She is an assistant professor at Kamakakūokalani Center for Hawaiian Studies at the University of Hawaiʻi at Mānoa. She earned her BA in Hawaiian studies with a minor in political science and a certificate in Hawaiian language. She also earned an MA and PhD in political science from the same institution. A longtime admirer of all things ulana lau hala, Keawe has now become a practitioner of this traditional and customary art form. Her narrative in this book is a reflection of that transformation.

Aunty Elizabeth Maluihi Lee, mānaleo (native speaker of Hawaiian) and master lau hala weaver, has been weaving since the age of six. Her work has been commissioned by and displayed at the Bishop Museum, Huliheʻe Palace, and at the Merrie Monarch Festival. In 1993, the Office of Hawaiian Affairs honored her as a living treasure of Hawaiʻi. To perpetuate the traditional art form of ulana lau hala, she created Ka Ulu Lauhala O Kona in 1996, a nonprofit organization that holds annual weaving conferences in Kailua, Kona.

Kaiwipunikauikawēkiu Lipe is a mother, wife, daughter, granddaughter, sister, aunty, hula dancer, and Native Hawaiian doctoral candidate in the College of Education in the Department of Education Administration at the University of Hawaiʻi at Mānoa (UHM). She is a 2013–2014 Kohala-Mellon doctoral fellow. Prior to that she was a graduate assistant with the W. K. Kellogg Foundation's Engaging Communities in Education initiative through Hawaiʻinuiākea School of Hawaiian Knowledge. Her prior experience includes service as the director of the Native Hawaiian Scholars Program at College Connections Hawaiʻi and the academic advisor for the Kawaihuelani Center for Hawaiian Language at UHM. She holds an MS in counseling psychology from Chaminade University of Honolulu (2008) and a BA in Hawaiian Studies from UHM (2005). She is also a graduate of Kamehameha Schools (2001) and a former Hawaiian immersion student.

Marsha MacDowell is professor of art and art history, Michigan State University; curator, Michigan State University Museum; core faculty member, MSU Museum Studies Program; and coordinator, Michigan Traditional Arts Program (a statewide partnership of the MSU Museum and the Michigan Council for the Arts and Cultural Affairs). Her research for many years has been largely focused on the documentation and analysis of the production, meaning, and use of traditional material culture; the development of educational resources and public arts policies related to traditional arts; the development of curriculum materials related to community-based knowledge; and the creation of innovative ways, including digital repositories, to increase access to and use of traditional arts materials. The overwhelming majority of her work has, by design and philosophy, been developed and implemented in collaboration with representatives of the communities and cultural groups whose cultural heritage it is focused on. She has led or co-led many local, state, and national research, publication, exhibition, education, festival program, and arts service projects focused on Native arts.

Marques Hanalei Marzan is a Hawaiian fiber artist born and raised in Kāne‘ohe, O‘ahu. He is highly experienced in his field and has learned and trained under noted experts in Hawai‘i, including master weavers Julia Minerva Kaawa and Esther Kakalia Westmoreland. Mr. Marzan continues to broaden his knowledge base of indigenous Pacific perspectives through his extensive travels. He has represented Hawai‘i in numerous gatherings of indigenous artists, including the Festival of Pacific Arts three times, held in Palau, American Samoa, and the Solomon Islands, and the Smithsonian Folklife Festival, in Washington, DC. Mr. Marzan is a staff member of the Bishop Museum's Cultural Resources Division, where he is able to provide greater opportunities for cultural practitioners to learn from the treasures of our past. He shares his understanding and passion for the fiber arts through public presentations, demonstrations, and workshops that restore, in modern culture, the living presence of rare Hawaiian forms, materials, and designs. Drawing upon this foundation of knowledge, Mr. Marzan bridges the traditions of the past with the innovations of the present, creating a dialogue within his work that speaks to the evolutionary continuity of culture.

Katherine Maunakea was a practitioner of ulana lau hala in addition to being a mānaleo (native speaker of Hawaiian), educator, composer, author, and historian who also practiced lā'au lapa'au (traditional Hawaiian medicine) and spiritual, physical, and cultural healing. In 1994, she received a Thomas Jefferson Award for her exceptional community leadership work. The National Library of Poetry published her poems in *Outstanding Poets of 1994.* That same year, she received the Ka Ha Mai Kalahikiola Nali'i'elua award from the Office of Hawaiian Affairs who designated her as a living treasure of Hawai'i. Her legacy continues to contribute to Hawai'i nei.

Jenna Robinson, although new to the poetry community, is no stranger to performing. Originally from Los Angeles, Jenna moved to Honolulu as an undergraduate at the University of Hawai'i at Mānoa. After the passing of her brother in 2010, Jenna taught herself how to play more than eight instruments and turned to open mic events for musical therapy. She quickly received recognition for her lyric skills and work ethic, as she performed around Honolulu, organized with multiple local youth nonprofits, and earned two undergraduate degrees at UH Mānoa, all before the age of twenty-one. She has performed in Hawai'i, California, New York City, Chicago, New Jersey, Tennessee, and recently in Charlotte, North Carolina, as a member of the 2012 Hawai'i Slam Team. As an up-and-coming local artist and educator, Jenna's goal is to find personal serenity in her own words as well as to inspire others to find happiness within themselves. You can still find her at UH Mānoa as a graduate student in the History Department, working toward educating others about the LGBT and African American experience in Hawai'i.

R. Kekeha Solis was born and raised in Honolulu. He is an assistant professor in Kawaihuelani Center for Hawaiian Language at the University of Hawai'i at Mānoa. Solis does research on 'ōlelo no'eau and language revitalization. His chapter highlights the brilliance of our kūpuna in weaving words.

Annette Ku'uipolani Wong was born and raised on the island of Ni'ihau. She is a native speaker and assistant professor at Kawaihuelani Center for Hawaiian Language. She earned a bachelor's degree in Hawaiian language, a master's degree in education in teacher education and curriculum studies, and a PhD in curriculum studies from the University of Hawai'i at Mānoa. She teaches Hawaiian language courses for Kawaihuelani Center for Hawaiian Language. Her research interests include Hawaiian language, culture, and language revitalization. One of her ongoing research projects is Wehe I Ka Pāpale, which focuses on the arts of lau hala. She has been collecting stories by interviewing master lau hala weavers throughout the state of Hawai'i who study the arts of lau hala from their kūpuna or family and who are extending the knowledge of weaving lau hala into the next generation.

Hawai'inuiākea Series

The Hawai'inuiākea Series provides a multidisciplinary venue for the work of scholars and practitioners from the Hawaiian community, a platform for thinkers and doers who grapple with real-world queries, challenges, and strategies. Each volume features chapters on a thematic topic from diverse fields such as economics, education, family resources, government, politics, health, history, land and natural resources, psychology, religion, and sociology. Each volume includes kupuna reflections, current viewpoints, and original creative expression.

No. 1   *I Ulu I Ke Kumu*, Puakea Nogelmeier, editor, 2011.
No. 2   *I Ulu I Ka 'Āina*, Jonathan K. Osorio, editor, 2013.

Proposals for volume themes may be submitted to:

Hawai'inuiākea School of Hawaiian Knowledge
Hawai'inuiākea Series
Office of the Dean
2450 Maile Way
Spalding 454
Honolulu, Hawai'i 96822

http://manoa.hawaii.edu/hshk/

Production Notes for Keawe, MacDowell, and Dewhurst | *'Ike Ulana Lau Hala*

Cover design by Mardee Melton

Composition by Westchester Publishing Services with display and text type in Palatino Linotype

Printing and binding by Sheridan Books, Inc.

Printed on 60 lb. House White, 444 ppi.